TOOL & DIE MAKER SECOND YEAR (PRESS TOOLS, JIGS & FIXTURES) DIES & MOULDS MCQ

OBJECTIVE QUESTION ANSWERS

MANOJ DOLE

Digitization is the need of the time. In the future, training in industrial training institutes will need to be conducted using online internet to make training more convenient and easy. E-books containing a set of MCQ questions will be made available to the trainees as they need to be more accustomed to the multiple choice questions MCQ to prepare for the online exams taking place in their industrial training institutes.

With all these factors in mind, Mr. Manoj Madhukar Dole Instructor, Industrial Training Institute, Satara, has written books according to the new annual system and NSQF-5 syllabus. And they've created theoretical mobile apps and blogs to make training easier, and made all these educational materials available for download on the world famous websites Google Play Store, Amazon and Apple Book Store.

The books were published by Hon'ble Joint Director Shri Rajendra Ghume Saheb Regional Office of Vocational Education and Training, Pune on 9/1/2019, at this time Shri Prakash Saigavkar Saheb Principal Government Industrial Training Institute Aundh Pune, Shri Tukaram Misal Saheb Principal Govt. Q. Sanstha Satara, Shri Sachin Dhumal Saheb District Vocational Education and Training Officer Satara, Shri Yatin Pargaonkar Saheb Principal Govt. Q. Sanstha Kolhapur, Shri Vikas Teke Saheb Inspector Vocational Education and Training Regional Office Pune, Palekar Foods Products Pvt. Ltd. Entrepreneurial Chairman of Satara Mr. Nilkanthrao Palekar Saheb, Chairman of Hira Foods Mr. Ibrahim Baba Tamboli Saheb, Mrs. Shalmali Pawar Headmaster Government Technical School Center Satara and other dignitaries were present on the occasion.

Contents

Prologue

Tool & Die Maker (Press Tools, Jigs & Fixtures) B is a simple Book for ITI Engineering Course Tool & Die Maker (Press Tools, Jigs & Fixtures) , Second Year, Sem- 3 & 4, Revised NSQ F-5 Syllabus in 2022, It contains objective questions with underlined & bold correct answers MCQ covering all topics including all about operation and programming of CNC turn centre and CNC machining centre to produce components, 2D & 3D machining with CAM software, Manufacture drill jig and fixture is also part of the practical. EDM & wire EDM operation to produce components, Construction of blanking and piercing tool, Basic construction of Hydraulic & Pneumatic circuits and basic functioning of electrical circuit and sensors, overhauling of different machines viz., drill, milling & lathe, Making of „V" bending tool and draw tool and lots more.

We add new question answers with each new version. Please email us in case of any errors/omissions. This is arguably the largest and best e-Book for All engineering multiple choice questions and answers.

As a student you can use it for your exam prep. This e-Book is also useful for professors to refresh material.

Foreword

Vocational education and training is imparted through the Department of Vocational Education and Training through the Department of Business Education and Business Practical to supply multi-skilled artisans in line with the rapidly growing demand in the industrial sector in the 21st century. All the occupations within the institutions are important, as the trainees from these occupations develop multi-skills as per the demands of the industry.

with the noble intention of making available MCQ e-books suitable for all businesses, considering that all the examinations in all the industries in the industrial sector are conducted online and include MCQ method questions. Mr. Manoj Madhukar Dole has written a very good e-book on MCQ method as per the new annual syllabus. This e-book will definitely be a guide for all the trainees, trainee candidates, training instructors and others concerned.

The author of the book is Mr. Manoj Madhukar Dole, Instructor Gov. ITI Satara has 17 years of training experience. Written as a new annual pattern, this e-book incorporates modern digital QR Code technology to understand the layout, simple language, and simple syntax, diagrams and videos for each subject. So I am sure that this e-book will definitely be useful for in-depth study and exam practice. The work they have done is certainly commendable.

Mr. Tukaram Misal
Principal Government Industrial Training Institute Satara.

Preface

DGET New Delhi and CSTARI Kolkata have been implementing an annual pattern for all businesses in ITI since the August 2018 session. The examination system will also be changed and it will be online from this year and since all the questions are of Objective Type (MCQ), the trainees are in dire need of in-depth study. It is with this in mind that we are delighted to present the books based on the old NIMI pattern and a complete overview of the new annual pattern, and we hope that these books will be a guide for all business directors and trainees. Is.

For writing these books, Johar Awate Saheb, Principal of ITI Akluj. Former Principal of ITI Satara Saigavkar Saheb, Assistant Director Shri Chandrakant Dhekne Saheb Regional Office of Vocational Education and Training, Pune, District Vocational Education and Training Officer Sachin Dhumal Saheb and Headmaster Government Technical School Kendra Shalmali Pawar Madam and son Adhiraj Dole, mother Kusum Dole, I am very grateful to my father Madhukar Dole and wife Ashwini Dole for their special guidance and cooperation from time to time.

Also, in a very short period of time, the book was reviewed by Shri Rajendra Ghume Saheb, Joint Director, Vocational Education and Training Regional Office, Pune, for his invaluable time in publishing the book. I am sincerely grateful for their feedback.

I am grateful to the Instructor of ITI Satara for there continuous support from the very beginning of writing the book.

From this book, I consider myself blessed to have shared my thoughts on e-learning with you. I will not claim that this book is perfect, because considering the perfection, this book is an attempt and is in its infancy. They will be valuable for improvement if they are tested and suggested.

Manoj Dole
Dated 9/1/2019

Acknowledgements

The industrial training and theoretical examination system of our industrial training institutes and these changes have been accepted by the craft instructors and the trainees. Theoretical examinations conducted in your industrial training institutes are also conducted online. Since these examinations are of multiple choice MCQ method, the trainees will need to get more practice of such questions.

With all these considerations in mind, Mr. Manoj Madhukar, Director, Dole Crafts, Katari Industrial Training Institute, Satara, has done a thorough study and with his diligent work and added his keen intellect, according to the new annual system and NSQF-5 syllabus, e-book of Katari and other machine trades. -Book) and they have created mobile apps and blogs on theoretical topics to make training easier and have made all these educational materials available for download on the world famous websites Google Play Store, Amazon and Apple Book Store. Training has been made easier by creating a print version and using advanced techniques like QR Code.

All these educational materials will definitely be a guide for all the trainees for in-depth study and for the craft instructors and other concerned who are imparting vocational training.

CHAPTER ONE

Tool & Die Maker Second Year MCQ Drawing

Online Test Exam
ITI Books
CNC Course
AutoCAD CAM
JOB & Apprentice
Online Theory
Computer Course
Trading Course
Web Designing
MSCIT Course
Shopping Business
Internet Business
Remotasks Course
Online Services
Top Sportsmans
Indian Army
Freedom Fighters
Top Scientists
Social Reformers
Motivational Speaker
Top Richest People
Join WhatsApp Group
Join Facebook Group
Like Facebook Page
PAN / Adhar / Licence Passport

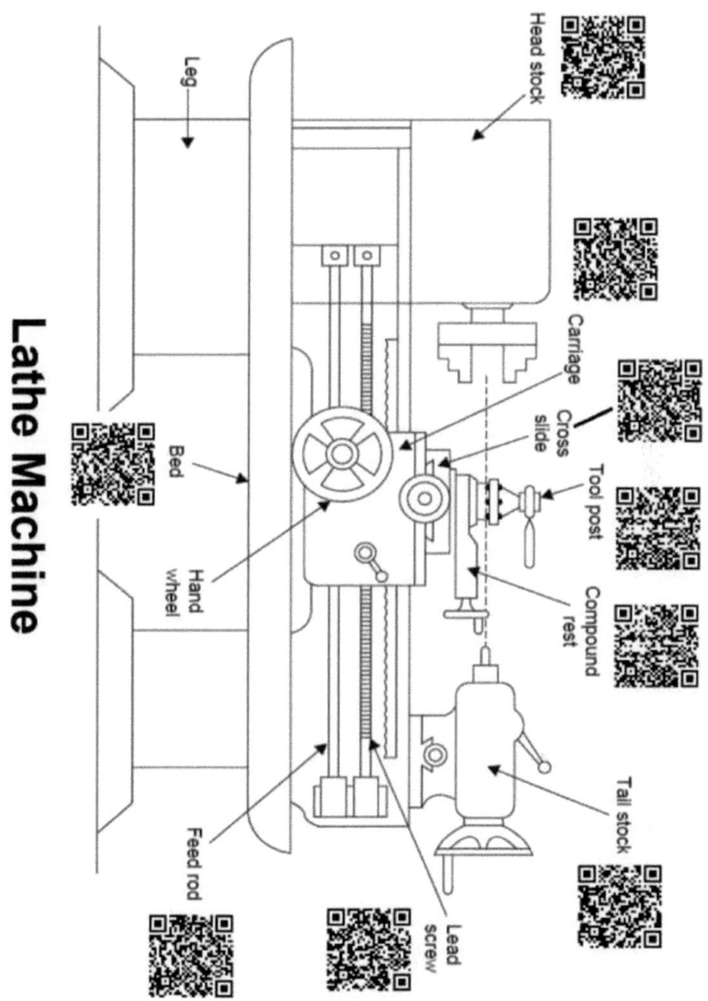
Lathe Machine
Head stock
Leg
Carriage
Cross slide
Tool post
Compound rest
Bed
Hand wheel
Tail stock
Feed rod
Lead screw

Bench Grinding Machine

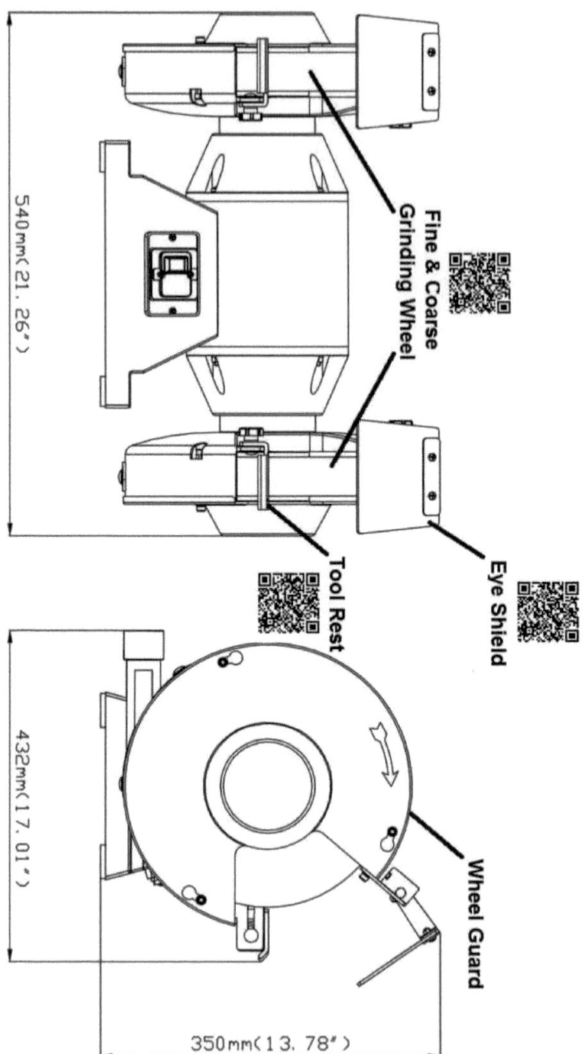

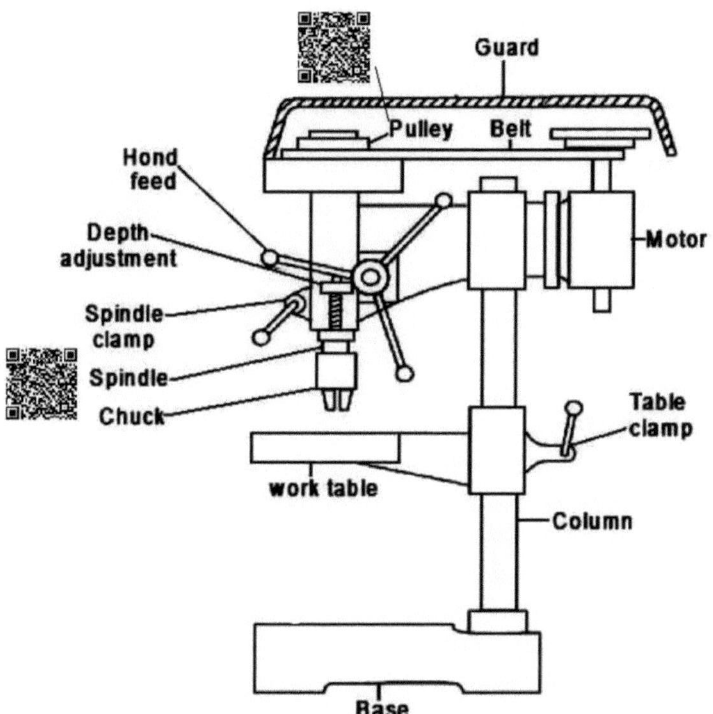

Piller Drilling Machine

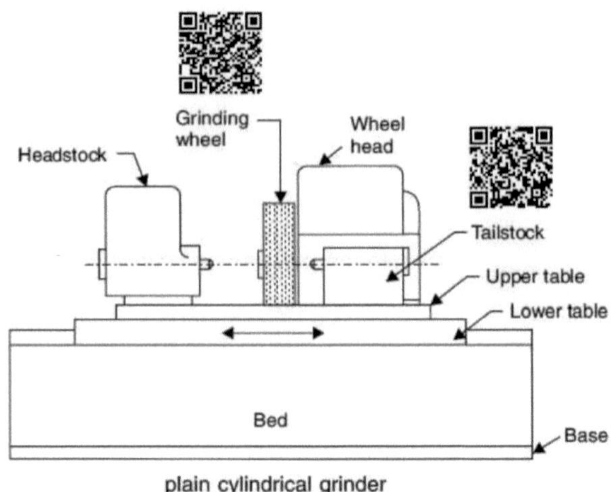

plain cylindrical grinder

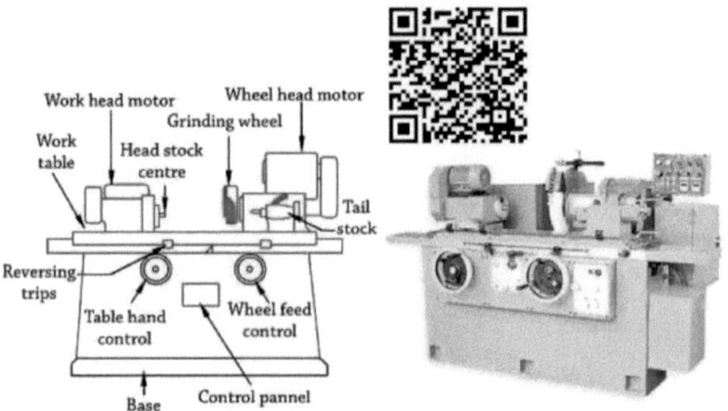

Cylindrical grinding machine

To study Different operations and parts of Surface Grinding Machine

SURFACE GRINDER

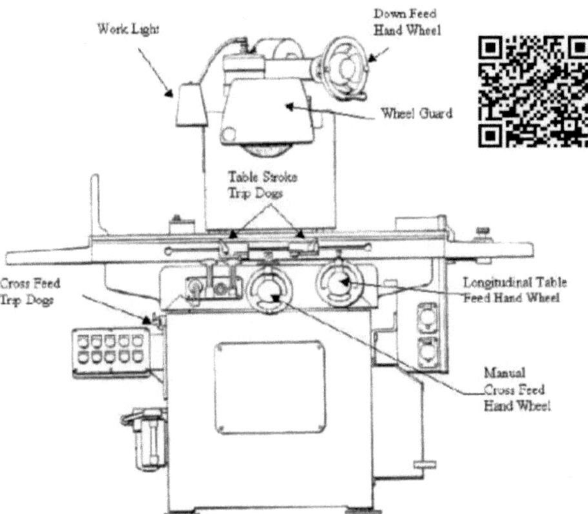

Surface grinding is used to produce a smooth finish on flat surfaces. It is a widely used abrasive machining process in which a spinning wheel covered in rough particles (grinding wheel) cuts

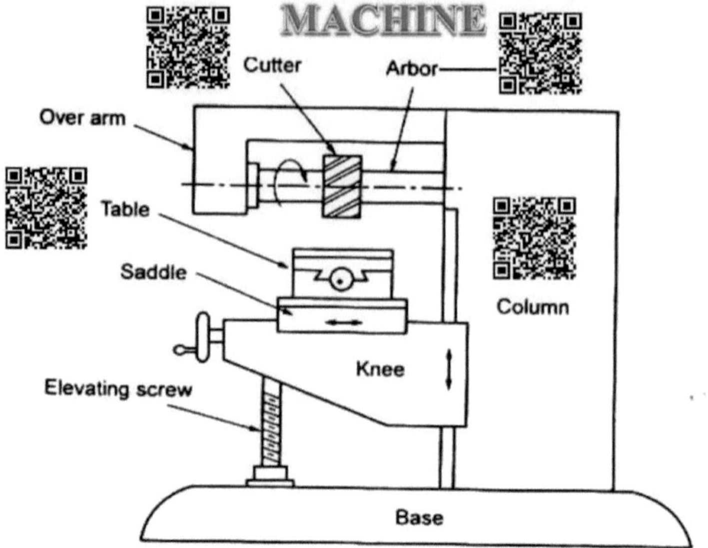
PLAIN OR HORIZONTAL MILLING MACHINE
Cutter
Arbor
Over arm
Table
Saddle
Column
Knee
Elevating screw
Base

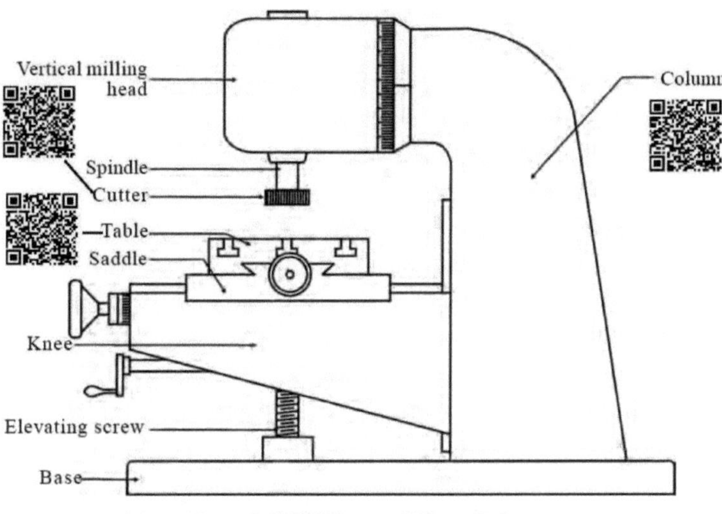

Vertical Milling Machine

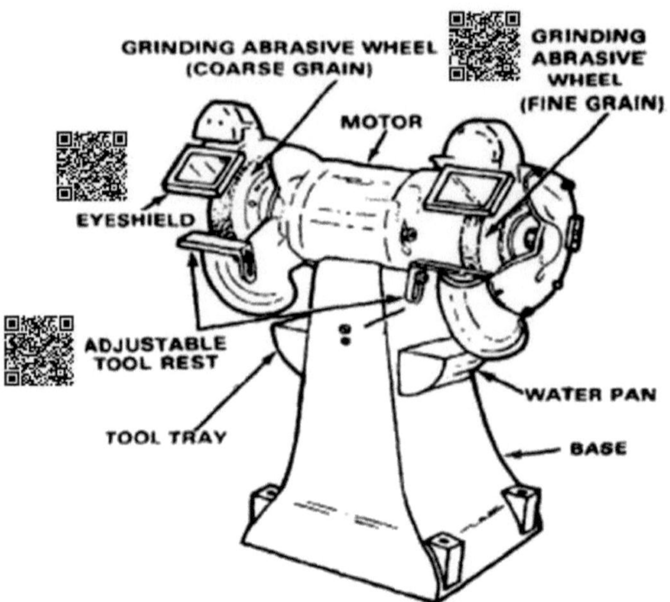

Pedastal Grinding Machine

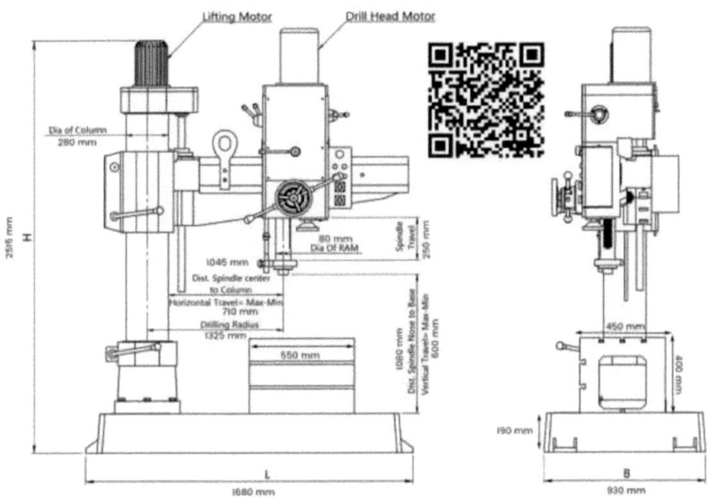

Radial Drilling Machine

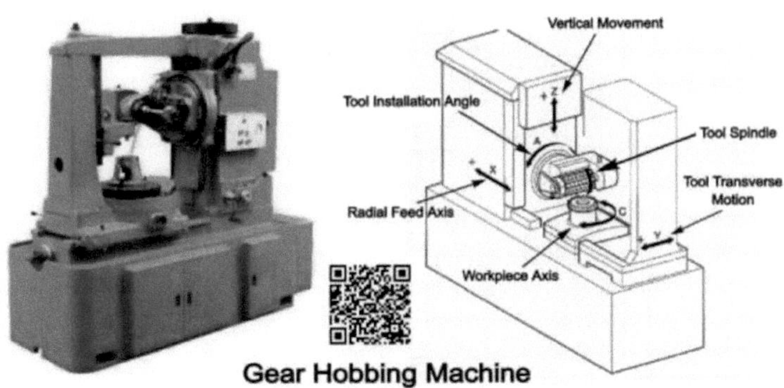

Gear Hobbing Machine

DOUBLE HOUSING PLANER

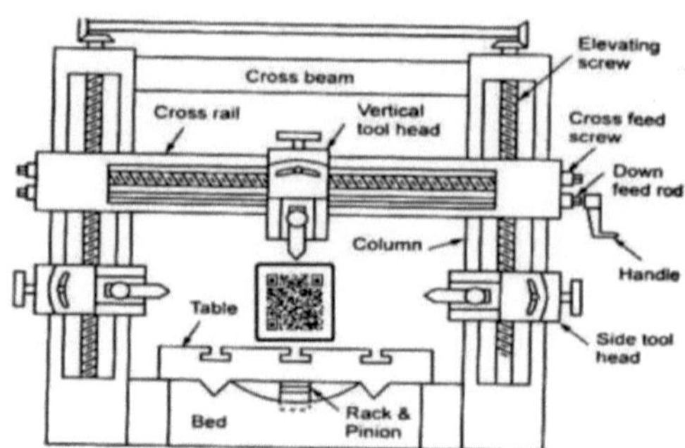

PIT PLANER

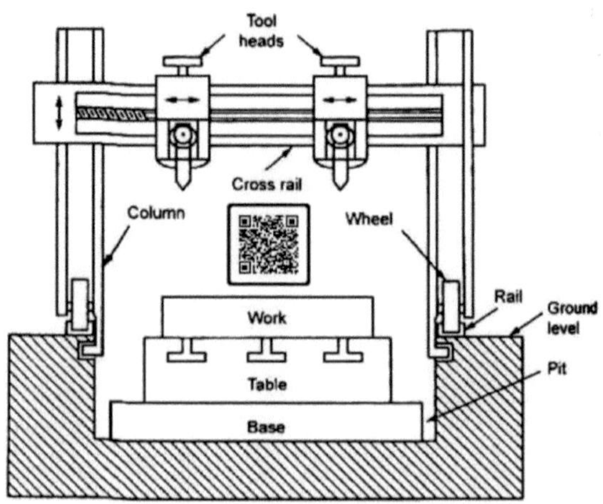

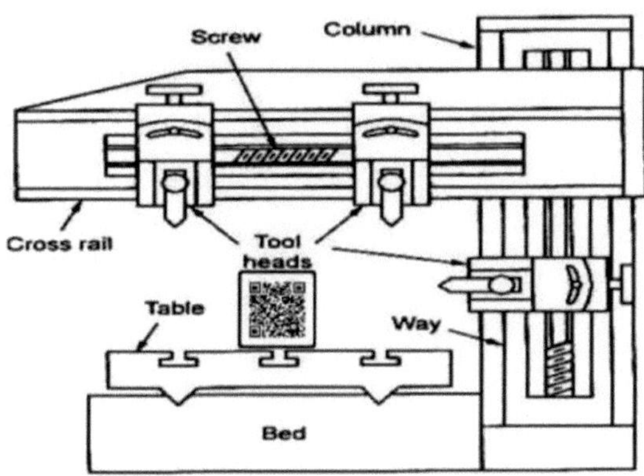

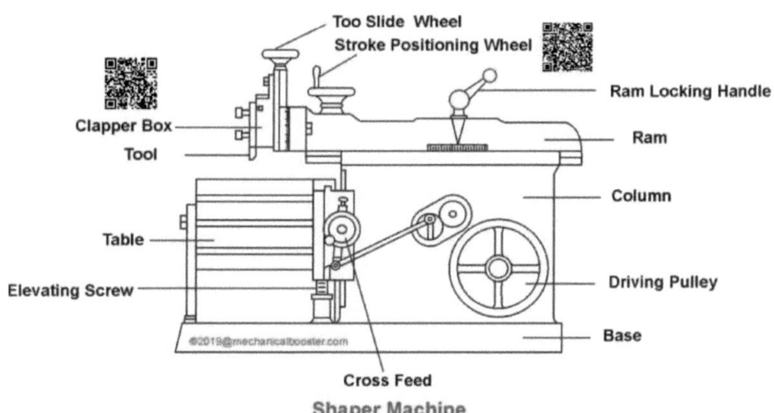

Shaper Machine

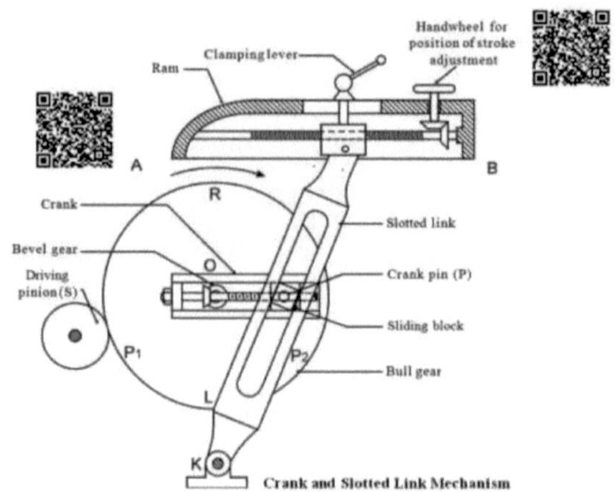

Quick Return Mechanism of Shaper Machine

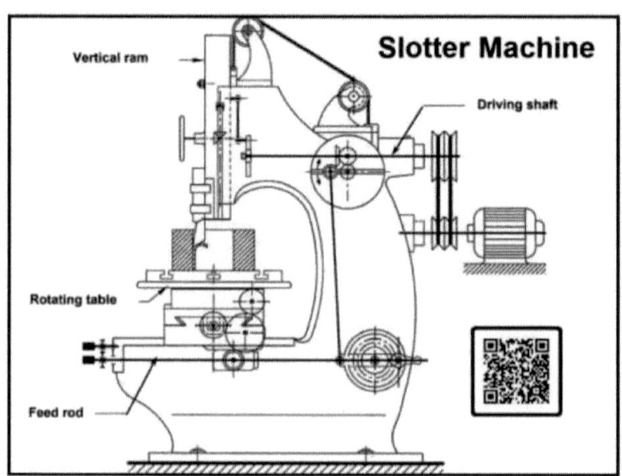

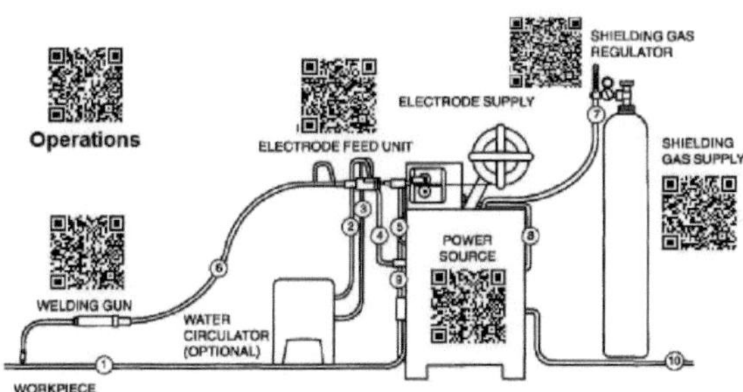

Gas Metal Arc Welding

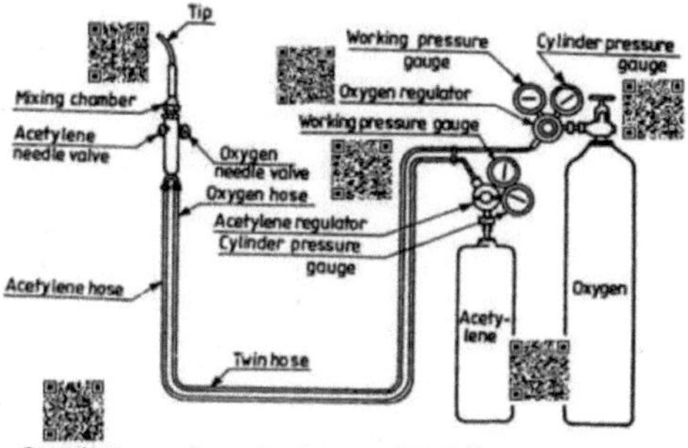

Oxy Acetylene Welding

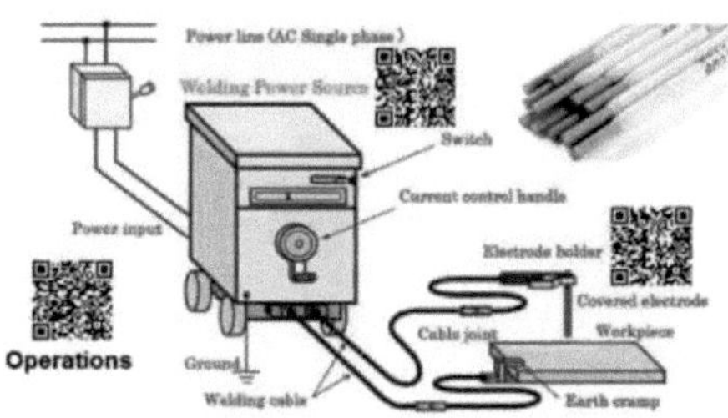

Shielded Metal Arc Welding

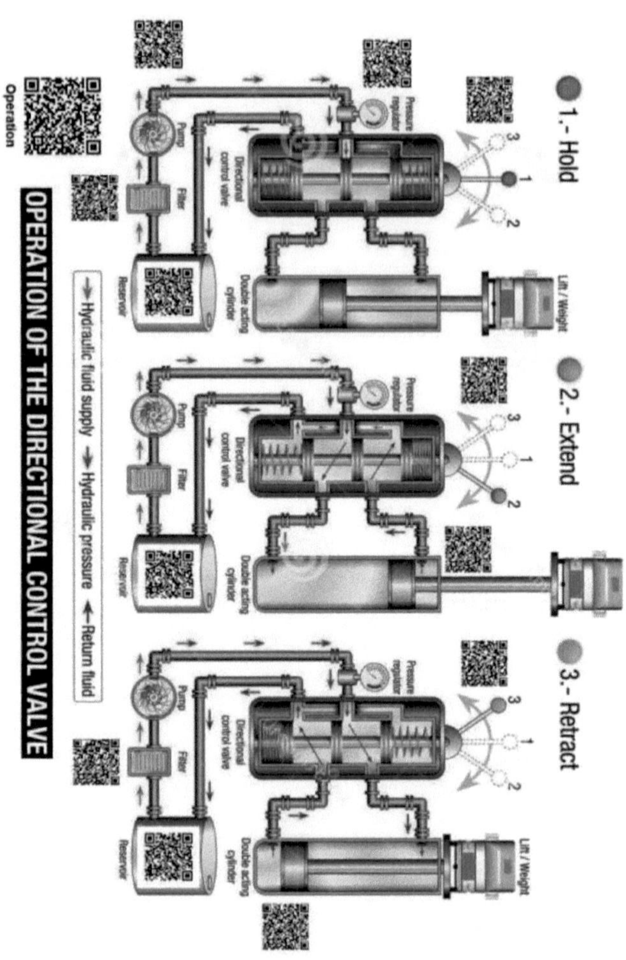
1.- Hold
2.- Extend
3.- Retract
Pressure regulator
Directional control valve
Pump
Filter
Reservoir
Double acting cylinder
Lift / Weight
Hydraulic fluid supply
Hydraulic pressure
Return fluid
OPERATION OF THE DIRECTIONAL CONTROL VALVE
Operation

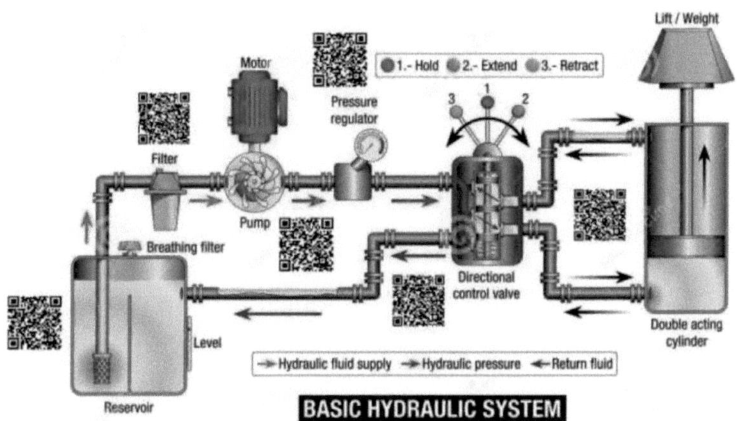

Direct Pressure Relief Valves

- The pressure relief valve provides protection against overload experienced by the actuators in a hydraulic system. One important function is to limit the force or torque produced by the hydraulic cylinders or motors.

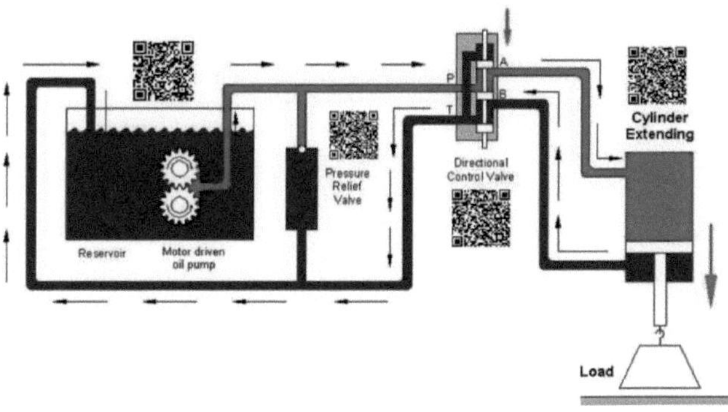

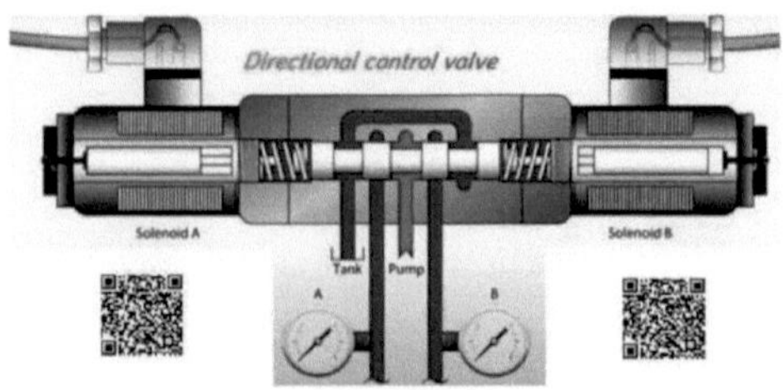
Directional control valve
Solenoid A
Solenoid B
Tank
Pump
A
B

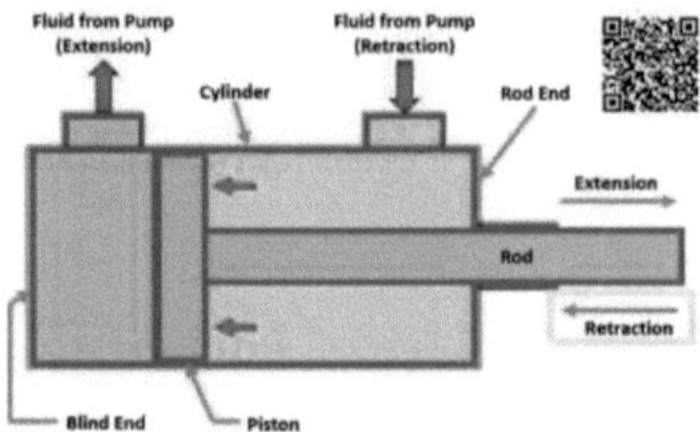
Double Acting, Single ended Cylinder
Fluid from Pump (Extension)
Fluid from Pump (Retraction)
Cylinder
Rod End
Extension
Rod
Retraction
Blind End
Piston

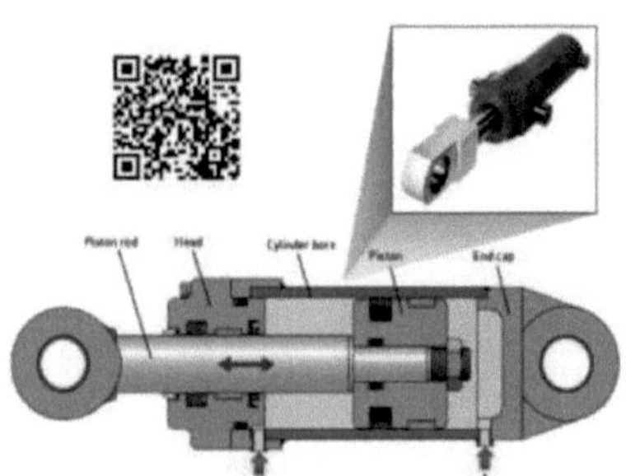
Hydraulic Cylinder

FLOW CONTROL VALVES

- A flow control valve can regulate the flow or pressure of the fluid.
- The fluid flow is controlled by varying area of the valve opening through which fluid passes.

GLOBE VALVE BUTTERFLY VALVE PLUG VALVE

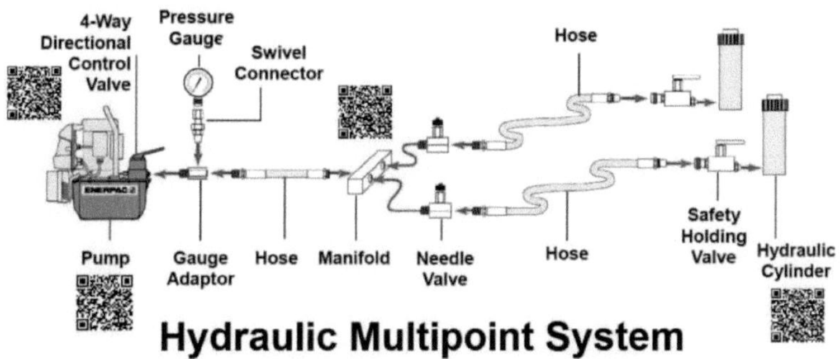

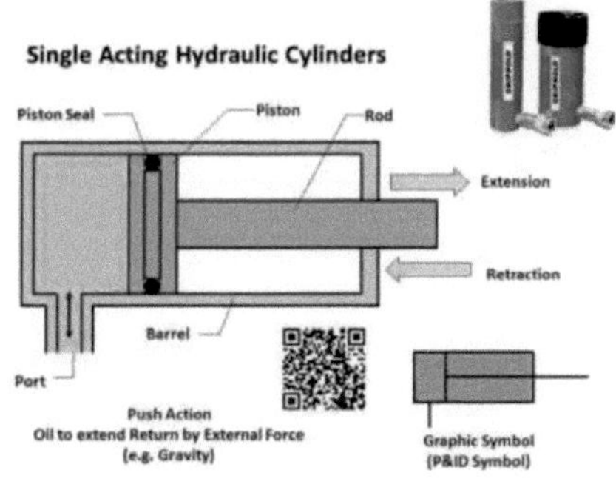

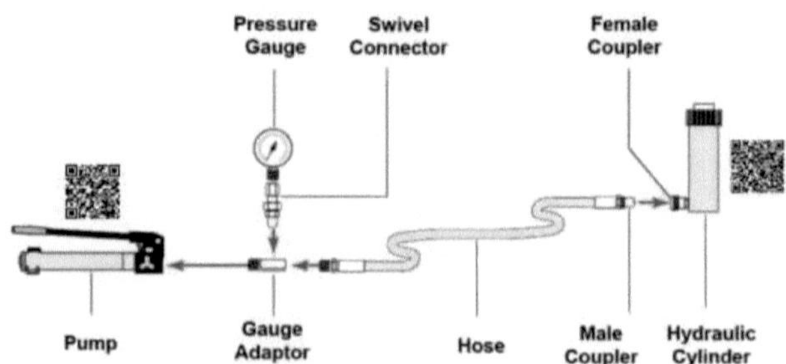
Pressure Gauge
Swivel Connector
Female Coupler
Pump
Gauge Adaptor
Hose
Male Coupler
Hydraulic Cylinder
Hydraulic Single Point System

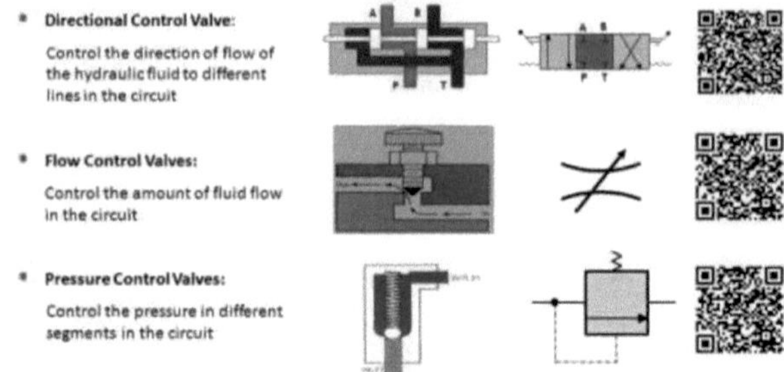
Types of Hydraulic Valves
Directional Control Valve:
Control the direction of flow of the hydraulic fluid to different lines in the circuit
Flow Control Valves:
Control the amount of fluid flow in the circuit
Pressure Control Valves:
Control the pressure in different segments in the circuit

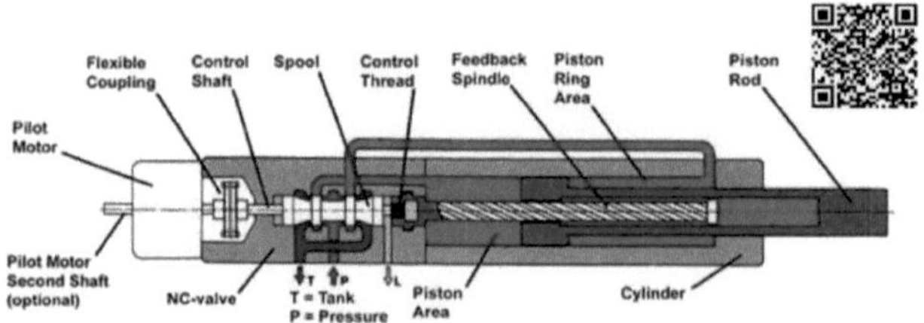
Hydraulic Valves - Parts and Components
Flexible Coupling
Control Shaft
Spool
Control Thread
Feedback Spindle
Piston Ring Area
Piston Rod
Pilot Motor
Pilot Motor Second Shaft (optional)
NC-valve
T = Tank
P = Pressure
Piston Area
Cylinder

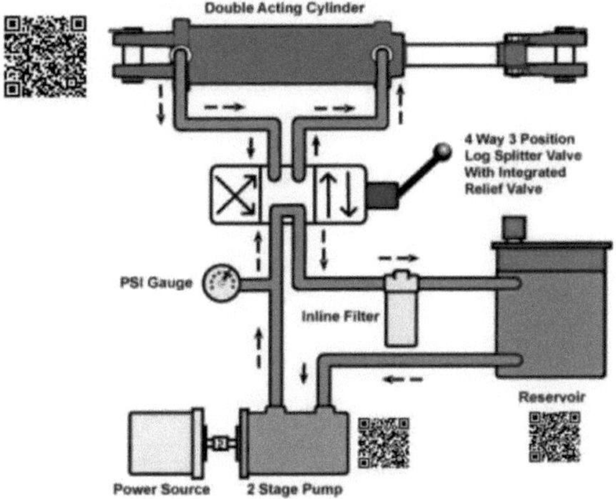

Hydraulic Double Acting Cylinder

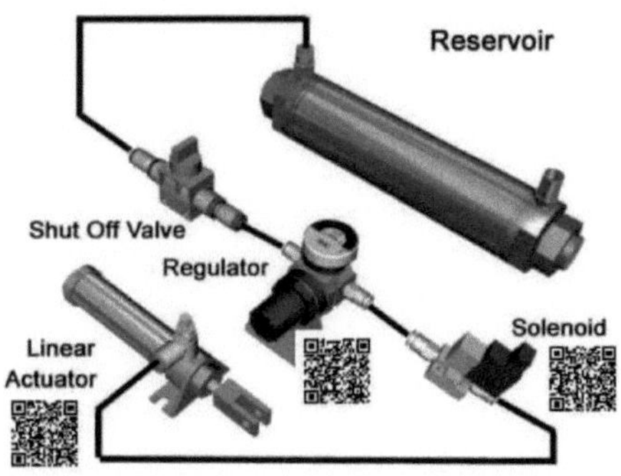

Pneumatic System

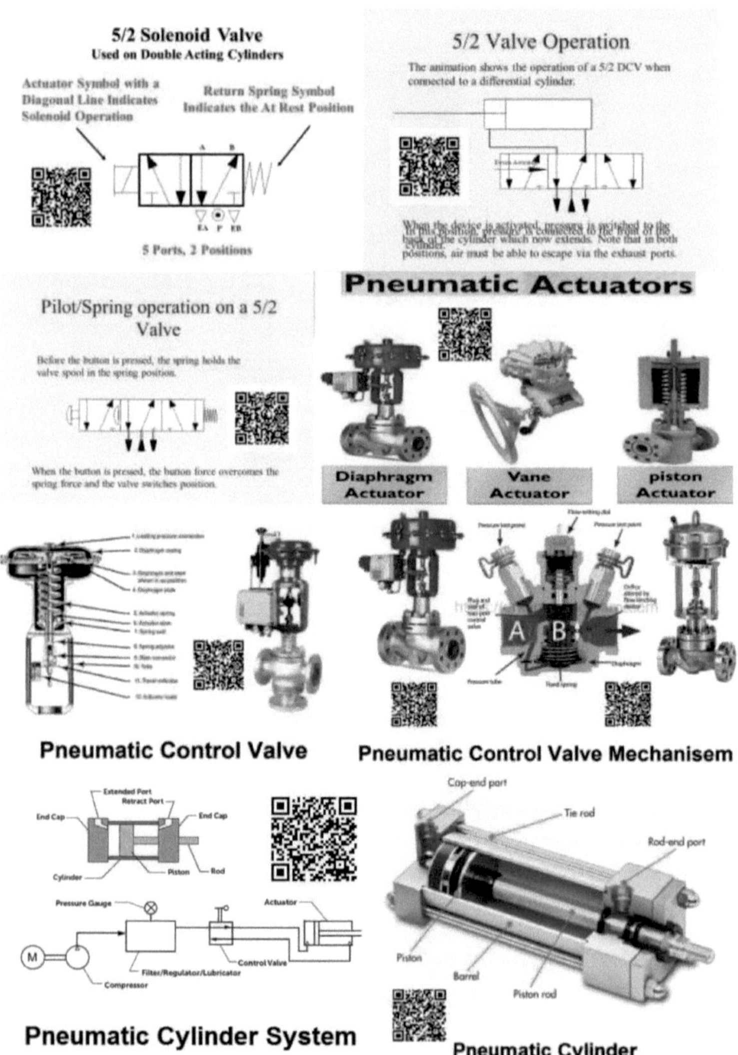
5/2 Solenoid Valve
Used on Double Acting Cylinders
Actuator Symbol with a Diagonal Line Indicates Solenoid Operation
Return Spring Symbol Indicates the At Rest Position
5 Ports, 2 Positions
5/2 Valve Operation
The animation shows the operation of a 5/2 DCV when connected to a differential cylinder.
Pneumatic Actuators
Pilot/Spring operation on a 5/2 Valve
Before the button is pressed, the spring holds the valve spool in the spring position.
When the button is pressed, the button force overcomes the spring force and the valve switches position.
Diaphragm Actuator
Vane Actuator
piston Actuator
Pneumatic Control Valve
Pneumatic Control Valve Mechanisem
Extended Port
Retract Port
End Cap
End Cap
Cylinder
Piston
Rod
Pressure Gauge
Actuator
Control Valve
Filter/Regulator/Lubricator
Compressor
Pneumatic Cylinder System
Cap-end port
Tie rod
Rod-end port
Piston
Barrel
Piston rod
Pneumatic Cylinder

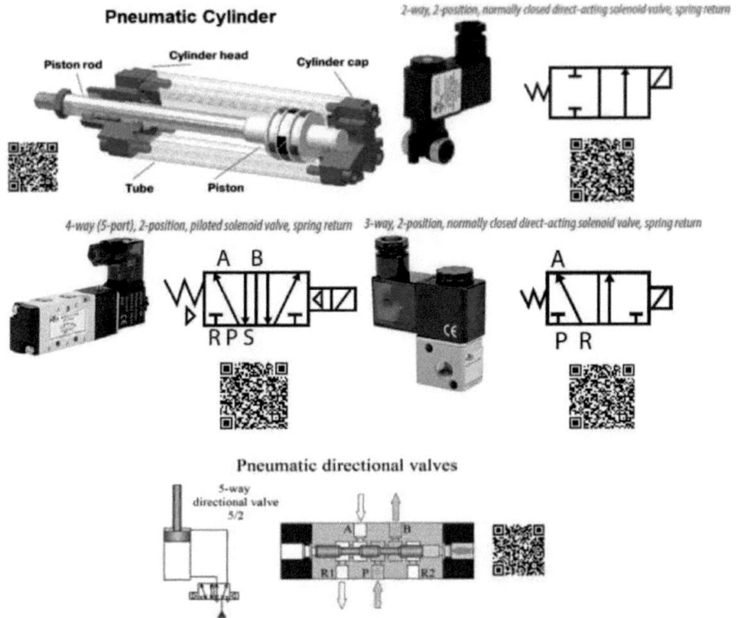
Pneumatic Cylinder
Piston rod
Cylinder head
Cylinder cap
Tube
Piston
2-way, 2-position, normally closed direct-acting solenoid valve, spring return
4-way (5-port), 2-position, piloted solenoid valve, spring return
A B
R P S
3-way, 2-position, normally closed direct-acting solenoid valve, spring return
A
P R
Pneumatic directional valves
5-way
directional valve
5/2
A
B
R1
P
R2

FRC Pneumatic System Layout
Air Tank
Limit Switch
Compressor
Air release valve
High Pressure (120psi)
Lower Pressure
Low Pressure (60psi or less)
Pressure regulator
Pressure regulator
Double solenoid valve
Solenoid valve

Pneumatic System
Air Tools
Air Tank
Pre-Filter
Final Filter
Air Hose
Manual Ball Valve
Filter/Regulator/Lubricator
Cylinder
Air Compressor
Air Dryer
Timer Drain Valve
Oil/Water Separator
Drip Leg Drain
Valve

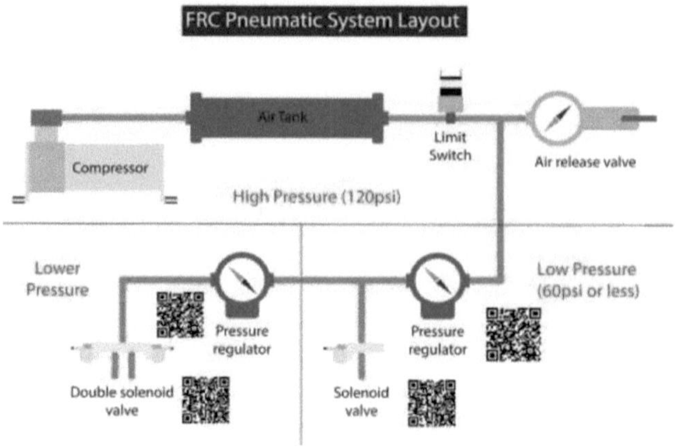

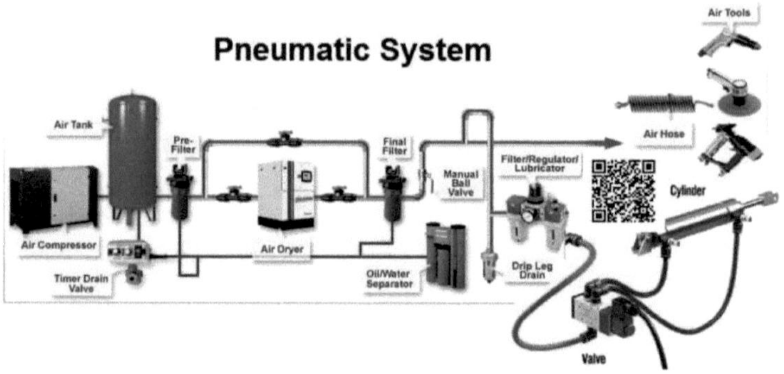

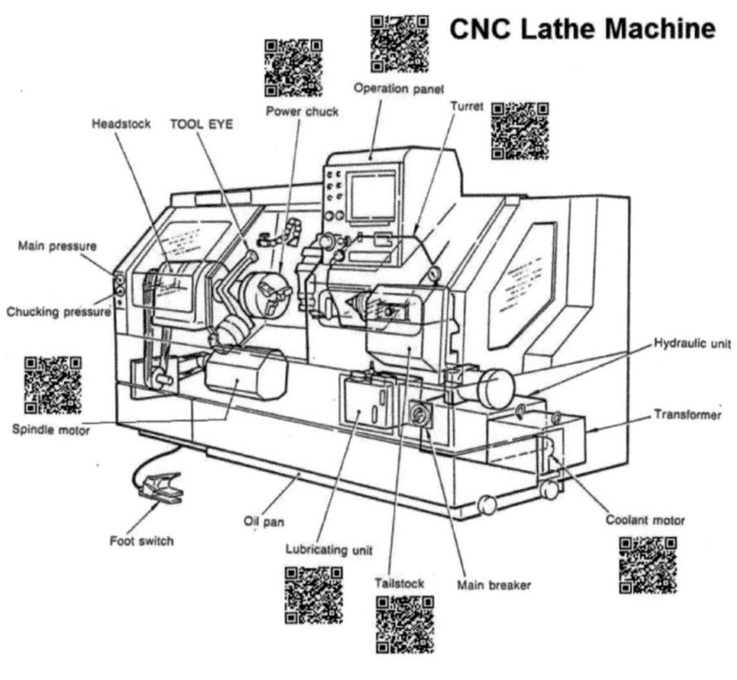
CNC Lathe Machine
Operation panel
Power chuck
Turret
Headstock
TOOL EYE
Main pressure
Chucking pressure
Hydraulic unit
Transformer
Spindle motor
Coolant motor
Oil pan
Foot switch
Lubricating unit
Tailstock
Main breaker

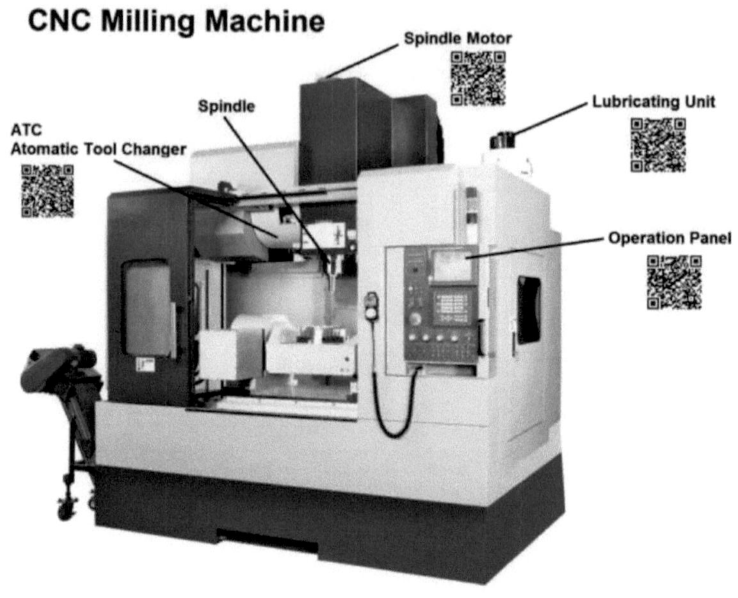

CNC Machine Power Pack

Tool Change & Spindle Speed in CNC Machine.

Coolant in CNC Machine.

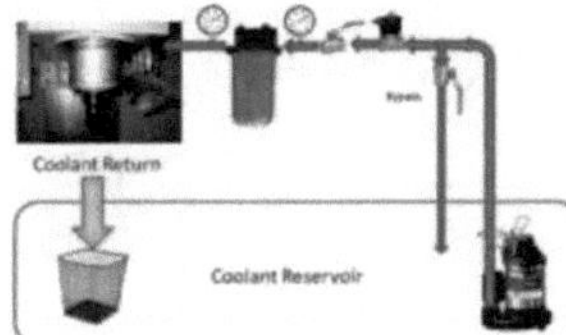

CHAPTER TWO

Tool & Die Maker Second Year MCQ

1] The jig bush used for drilling and reaming of a hole is...?

A] Press fit bush

B] Liner bush

C] Slip renewable bush

D] Fixed renewable bush

2] The following given which device is used for holding job & guide for toll while working?

A] Gauge

B] Housing

C] Jig

D] Fixture

3] The following given device which one for used clamping job only?

A] Jig

B] Fixture

C] Housing

D] Gauge

4] While fabricated by welding job which device is used for holding fixed or revolving if necessary up to 360°C of welding job?

A] Gauge

b] Template

C] Jig

D] Fixture

5] The main things of drilling jig its not clamping with machine table which reason is correct given following?

A] it is strong for operation

B] it is easy for operation

C] many different size holes produce by different setting while drilling on job

D] for this device has lot of time

6] Following which locations is most usefull for round shape job location?

A] pin type locator

B] wedge type locator

C] vee locator

D] adjustable stop locators

7] Following which reason is correct for using bushing in drilling jigs?

A] easy for drilling

B] for fixed drill hole size

C] for accurate drilling operation

D] for given better finish drilling hole

8] The metal for manufacturing jig bush is...?

A] mild steel

B] cast iron

C] cast steel

D] tool steel

9] Given following bush which busing used for locating renewable bushing?

A] press fit bushing

B] linear bushing

C] special bushing

D] knurd bushing

10] jig has tolerance..?

A] five present of job tolerance

B] ten percent of job tolerance

C] 20% to 50% of job tolerance

D] 100% of job tolerance

Jig

11] Following which jig is use for location from bore?
A] plate jig
B] solid jig
C] post jig
D] box jig
12] Following which jig having drill plate?
A] solid jig
B] plate jig
C] box jig
D] table jig
13] Following which locator is used for internal diameter location?
A] solid saports
B] Pin type locator
C] Vee locator
D] nest locator
14] Drm jig bushing-are generally hardened to -----------]
A] Mild steel
B] Cast iron
C] Cast steel
D] Tooi steel
15] Jigs is device which -------------
A] Locate the work piece
B] Holding and supporting the work piece
C] Guide the cutting tool
D] Does all the above

Fixture

16] Which among the following jigs is used forllocation from a bore?

A] Plate jig

B] Solid jig

C] Post jig

D] Box jig

17] Fixture is a production device which -----------]

A] Holds and locate the work piece

B] Holds the piece

C] Chats the work piece,

D] Neither holds nor]Locates the-work piece

18] Which one of the following is used to guide tool and hold the job in mass production? '

A] Gauge]

B] Housing

C] Fixture

D] Jig

19] Which among the following is the purpose for proi/iding bushing in a drill jig?

A] For locating accurately and guiding the drill for precise drilling operation

B] For determining the size of the hole to be drilled

C] For easy drilling

D] For getting good finished surface in the drilled holes

20] Drill jig are used for? _

A] Drill operations only]

B] Clamping the job for drilling

C] Drilling, Reaming, Tapping and other operations

D] Guiding the tools only

21] Which one of the following jigs consists of drill plate, which rests on the component to be drilled?]]]]

A] Solid jig]

B] Plate jig]

C] Box jig

D] Trunnion jig

22] Jig is a device which -----------

A] Locates the work piece]

B] Hold and supports the work piece and guides tool

C] Guides the cutting tool

D] Hold the cutting tool]

23] Drill jig are used for ....]

A] Drilling, reaming, tapping and other allied operations

B] Drilling operations only

C] Clamping the job when drilling

D] Guiding the tool only

24] Fixture is a production device which---------: -----

A] holds the work piece '

B] Locate the work piece

C] Holds and locates the work piece

D] Neither holds nor locates the work piece

25] Purpose of the Box Jig is to

A] Hold the job and guide the tool to produce internal threads

B] To produce many inclined holes

C] To produce many straight holes

D] None of these

26] Jigs and fixtures are --------]

A] Machining tools

B] Precision tools

C] Both (a] & (b]

D] None of these

27] 'How jig are in terms of weight compared to fixtures?

A] Jigs are lighter than fixtures

B] Jigs are heavier than fixtures

C] jigs are equal in weight to fixtures for same operation

D] None of these

28] Which fixtures are used for machining parts which musthav-e machined details evenw spaced?

A] Profile fixtures

B] Duplex fixtures

<u>C] Indexing fixtures</u>

D] None of these

Indexing head

29]What is the profile of the knife cutting edge of the upper blade of the hand level shear?

A] <u>curved</u>

B] straight

C] inclined

D] beveled

CNC Machine Tape Punch

image

30] Tape punch having 1 inch in width tape it is made by

A] Paper Mylar

B] Aluminum Mylar

C] Plastic

D] Above all

31] In point two point positioning positioning system........] Is acceptable

A] Open loop control system

B] Closed loop control system

C] Above both

D] None of them

32] In CNC machine having.......

A] Lead screw

B] Ball lead screw

C] Above both

D] None of both

CNC Program Coordinate

image

33] The aim of sub program is........

A] For find coordinates X Y Z.

B] For other small machine.

C] To avoid cutting tool nose tool nose penetration in Jobs surface of high speed.

D] While machining of job in special condition do not use time to time of program block.

34] What is mean by while while xyz co-ordinate point measure zero-measurement

A] Reference mark.

B] Work zero

C] Co-ordinate points

D] Above all

35] CNC machine specified by axis……

A] 2 axis

B] 3 axis

C] 4 axis

D] Above all

CNC Machine Axis

image

36] Xyz axis of CNC machines which point is used for measurements.

A] Work zero point

B] Machine zero point

C] Common zero point

D] Above all

37] Following which point is not useful in CNC machine.

A] various operation done on CNC machine.

B] Less amount for inspection.

C] Hard for setting measure.

D] Machine efficiency is depend upon operators skill.

38] For selection of zero offset before necessary..........

A] cutter is fixed on machine table.

B] The data entered in machine.

C] Job is fixed on machine table.

D] Speed and feed selection necessary before machine operates.

CNC Work Zero Offset Setting.

image

39] In zero offset program indicates........] Code of following

A] X y z

B] X0 y0 z00

C] X10 Y20 Z30

D] G71

40] Work zero is

A] Datum of machine zero on job position.

B] Indicate by X0Y0Z0.

C] Selection of point on job according to program.

D] The end of machining point

41] M command is used for starting operation and complete revolution cycle M03 means.

A] Stop the program.

B] Program completed and reset.

C] Complete the program.

D] Spindle clockwise motion.

CNC Machine Power Pack

image

42] CNC machine is not manually operated it is control by...........

A] Program

B] operation

C] Cam

D] Plug board system

43] In CNC machine M13 means

A] coolant stop

B] coolant on

C] spindle stop

D] coolant on & spindle on

44] The function of power pack in CNC machine.

A] For balancing of lubricants heat.

B] For increasing heat of lubricants.

C] For destroy heat of lubricant.

D] Above all.

<u>CNC Machine Bed.</u>

image

45] The section of CNC machine bed is.....

A] Flat

B] Half round

<u>C] Rectangular</u>

D] Triangular

46] Following which statement is disadvantage of CNC machine.

A] Less inspection charge.

B] Less tooling charge.

C] Increase production rate.

<u>D] High establishment charge.</u>

47] The point to point system is more effective for......

A] Turning

B] Profile milling

C] Grinding

<u>D] Drilling</u>

<u>Tool Setting on NC Machine.</u>

image

48] Tool setting on NC machine on......] unit.

A] Presetting device.

B] Order special device without machine.

C] On n c machine other empty time.

D] When other operation working on machine.

49] For measuring system having built-in coordinates in this system..........] is called zero position.

A] Reference point.

B] Machine zero point.

C] Work zero point

D] Program zero point.

50] Job turning on CNC machine 50 mm dia turn with programs said the trial run 50.1 mm at production time following which Idea used for correct dia making

A] by increase offset of tool 0.1 mm.

B] by increase offset of tool 0.05 mm

C] by decrease offset of tool 0.05 mm

D] by decrease offset of tool 0.1 mm

CNC Copying Lathe Machine.

image

51] For measure zero offset dim dimensions on CNC machine.........mode is set

A] MDI

B] Jog

C] Automatic

D] preset

52] Coping unit of copying lathe is work on

A] Mechanical power system

B] Hand power system

C] Hydraulic power system

D] None of them

53] Following which advantage of Pneumatic power system

A] For increase production rate.

B] Less cash for layout

C] Good climate for work

D] Above all

Principle of CNC Machine Templates.

image

54] For face copying........] Type template is used

A] Rounded

B] Plate type

C] Flat

<u>D] Triangular</u>

55]............] Is Main principle of CNC MACHINE?

A] Indicate all states in numbers

B] More time required for mechanical control on machine.

C] Cutting speed is more than manual control.

<u>D] Production sequence in workshop is stored by block number in machine.</u>

56] For copy of one shaft.......] Type template is used.

<u>A] Rounded</u>

B] Triangular

C] Flats

D] Square

<u>CNC Program Tool Path.</u>

image

57] The symptoms of continuous path is

A] Called counting system.

B] Tool and work piece on co-ordinate Axis for inter related motion.

C] By the setting of cutter feed and speed

D] Above all

58] Misc command M30 means........

A] End of program and reset

B] Program stop

C] Clockwise motion of spindle

D] Complete the programs

59] Following which affect on milling surface while by milling with unsetting spindle vertical milling machine with- longitudinal feed.

A] Convex surface

B] Concave surface

C] Radius cross line

D] Rough surface

CNC Milling Operation]

image

60] While milling by vertical milling machine with 12 mm dia end mill cutter through slot provide on mild steel plate the cutter is sleep and broken for this fault how it is avoid.

A] High speed spindle

B] Low cutting speed

C] Increase of cut depth

D] Less the depth and feed of cutter

61] Having 5 mm pitch of screw and dividing ratio of 40 : 1 what is lead of milling machine

A] 0.25 mm

B] 5 mm

C] 8 mm

D] 200 mm

62] If not use of backlash Eliminator slap cutter used for down milling operation which safety to be observed?

A] Less lead and depth

B] High lead

C] high lead and less depth

D] High lead and high speed

CNC Machine Zero & Feed Rate.

cnc machine zero.PNG

63] Zero offset is the distance between.....] And.........

A] G41 & g42

B] Machine zero & work zero

C] Reference point and tapping mode

D] None of them

64] The feed rate is programmed as mm per minute with G ....] And mm per- Revolution with G.

A] G41 & g42

B] G 43 and G 40

C] G 94 and g95

D] None of them

65] For collection all instructions from.......] In CNC control unit

A] Memory

B] Tape reader

C] Control panel

D] Operator

CNC Drilling Machine.

cnc drilling machine.jpg

66] For control forward and backward of- CNC drilling machine y axis.........

A] Spindle

B] Table

C] Clockwise

D] Column

67] M 01 command means.....

A] For stopping programs

B] End of program and reset

C] Stopping programs condition

D] Clockwise rotation of machine spindle

68] CNC machine is founded by American scientist john person in.......] Year

A] 1950

B] 1952

C] 1955

D] 1957

CNC Control, Input & Memory Unit.

cnc control.jpg

69] Name of unit used to command the CNC machine.

A] Control unit

B] Memory unit

C] Input unit

D] Output unit

70] Name of unit used to processing the data in CNC machine.

A] Memory unit

B] Control unit

C] Input unit

D] Output unit

71] Name of unit used to storing the data in CNC machine.

A] Input unit

B] Control unit

C] Memory unit

D] Output unit

Servo Motor in CNC Machine.

servo motor.jpg

72] Name of unit used to calculation of data in CNC machine.

A] Output unit

B] Arithmetic unit

C] Memory unit

D] Input unit

73] Name of unit used to display result of processing data in CNC machine

A] Arithmetic unit

B] Output unit

C] Memory unit

D] Input unit

74] Servo Motor in CNC machine is used to.............

A] Changing tool on machine spindle

B] Driving machine spindle

C] Fixing job on machine spindle

D] Proving job on spindle

Types of CNC Machine.

types of cnc.jpg

75] One of the below part of CNC machine used to changing tools on spindle.

A] Servo Motor

B] Control panel

C] Automatic tool changer A T C

D] High speed spindle

76] One of the below CNC machine in CNC milling category is.......

A] Chucking centre

B] CNC late

C] Vertical machining centre

D] Surface grinding machine

77] One of the below CNC machine in turning centre or CNC lathe category is.......

A] Vertical machining centre

B] Horizontal machining centre

C] Vertical turning centre

D] Profile grinding machine

Miscellaneous Functions for CNC Machine.

miscellaneous function.jpg

78] One of the below CNC machine in grinding Centre category is.....

A] Universal milling centre

B] Cylindrical grinding machine

C] CNC late

D] Vertical machining centre

Grinding Wheel

79] In CNC Machine programming word M indicates

A] Feed rate

B] Spindle speed

C] Miscellaneous function

D] Tool number

80] In CNC Machine programming preparatory function G00 is for.....

A] Linear interpolation

B] Clockwise circular interpolation

C] Counter clockwise circular interpellation

D] Hold

Preparatory Functions for CNC Machine.

preparatory function.jpg

81] In CNC Machine programming preparatory function G02 is for.....

A] Linear interpolation

B] Clockwise circular interpolation

C] Counter clockwise circular interpellation

D] Hold

82] One of the bellow preparatory function G 00 is used in CNC program for.........

A] Linear interpellation or feed motion in straight line.

B] Clockwise circular interpellation

C] Point to point Positioning or Rapid motion.

D] Counter clockwise circular interpellation

83] One of the bellow preparatory function used in CNC program for 3D interpellation

A] G 05

B] G12

C] G17

D] G18

Threading & Tapping on CNC Machine.

threading & tapping on cnc.jpg

84] One of the bellow preparatory you function used in CNC program for thread cutting constant lead

A] G33

B] G40

C] G53

D] G62

85] One of the bellow preparatory function used in CNC program for tapping operation.

A] G-40

B] G53

C] G62

D] G63

86] One of the below preparatory function used in CNC program for milling operation.

A] G62

B] G63

C] G 78, 79

D] G81

Drilling, Boring & Reaming on CNC Machine

drilling boring & reaming.jpg

87] One of the bellow preparatory function used in CNC program for drilling operation.

A] G 81

B] G 82

C] G 84

D] G 85

88] One of the bellow preparatory function used in CNC program for reaming operation.

A] G 84

B] G 85

C] G 86

D] G 90

89] One of the below preparatory function used in CNC program for boring operation.

A] G 86

B] G 90

C] G 91

D] G 92

CNC Program Sequence Number.

cnc program sequence.png

90] In CNC program which letter is used to indicate the sequence number of the block

A] N

B] G

C] F

D] S

91] In CNC program which letter is used to indicate position of linear axis

A] ABC

B] UVW

C] XYZ

D] IJK

92] One of the below letters used in CNC program for Feed rate

A] S

B] F

C] T

D] M

Tool Change & Spindle Speed in CNC Machine.

tool change i cnc.jpg

93] One of the below letters used in CNC program for spindle speed in RPM

A] M

B] T

C] S

D] F

94] In CNC program which letter is used to indicate TOOL function number of tool

A] T

B] S

C] M

D] F

95] In CNC program which miscellaneous function used to program stop

A] M03

B] M00

C] M01

D] M02

CNC Machine Spindle Direction.

cnc machine spindle direction.png

96] One of the below miscellaneous function used to program optional Stop

A] M 01

B] M 02

C] M 03

D] M 04

97] In CNC program miscellaneous function M02 is used to......

A] Program stop

B] Optional program stop

C] End of program

D] Clockwise spindle on

98] In CNC program miscellaneous function M03 is used to..........

A] Counter clockwise spindle on

B] Clockwise spindle on

C] Spindle off

D] Tool chang

Coolant in CNC Machine.

coolant in cnc machine.jpg

99] One of the below miscellaneous function used in CNC program for spindle stop.

A] M04

B] M05

C] M06

D] M07

100] In CNC program which miscellaneous function is used for Tools change

A] M06

B] M07

C] M09

D] M10

101] One of the below miscellaneous function used in CNC program for coolant on

A] M08

B] M09

C] M10

D] M11

Clamping the Job on CNC Machine.

clamping the job on cnc.jpg

102] One of the below miscellaneous function in CNC program used for coolant off

A] M11

B] M10

C] M9

D] M15

103] In CNC program which miscellaneous function used for clamping the job on machine table.

A] M09

B] M10

C] M11

D] M15

104] One of the below miscellaneous function in CNC program used for unclamp the job

A] M11

B] M15

C] M30

D] M60

Work piece change in CNC Machine.

workpice change in cnc.jpg

105] In CNC program which miscellaneous function used for change of workpiece

A] M30

B] M60

C] M68

D] M78

106] The machine is.........for zero off-setting on CNC Machine.

A] In MDI Mode

B] In JOG Mode

C] In Automatic Mode

D] In Present Mode

107] The feed rate on NC Machine is indicate by ......code.

A] X

B] Y

C] F

D] Z

CNC Machine Axis Position]

cnc machine axis position.jpg

108] The position of axis is indicate by.......code.

A] X,Y,Z

B] P,Q,R

C] A,B,C

D] M,N,O

109] CNC Drilling Machine is on.......Axis Programmed.

A] Two Axis

B] Three Axis

C] Four Axis

D] Six Axis

110] From.......unit collect instruction in control unit of CNC

A] Machine Tool

B] Instruction

C] Magnetic Box

D] Memory

Working Graph of CNC Machine]

working graph of cnc machine.jpg

111] For preparing tape of NC Machine----------code is used.

A] EIA Code

B] ISO Code

C] ASC Code

D] None of them.

112] CNC Machine gives more accurate production than convention machine, But it is more expensive because.

A] It has AC cabin

B] It has dust proof cabin

C] It has strong foundation

D] It has more space

113] CNC Machine is working on graphical base the point on digital line, indicated digital points call..........

A] Graph

B] Input Media

C] Co-Ordinate

D] Original Point

Axis Rotary Motion in CNC Machine]

axis rotary motion in CNC.png

114] On CNC Machine for longitudinal feed has.......axes, cross feed......axis and for vertical feed........axis name given.

A] A,B,C

B] X,Y,Z

C] P,Q,R

D] M,N,O

115] For rotary motion CNC machine axis has.......name given.

A] A,B,C

B] X,Y,Z

C] P,Q,R

D] M,N,O

116] CNC Machine means.......

A] Natural Control Machine

B] Pneumatic control Machine

C] Numerical Control Machine

D] No Command Machine

117] The inner formers of a hydraulic pipe bending machine are able to bend pipes up to a diameter of

A] 40mm

B] 100mm

C] 20mm

D] 75mm

118] Which is not the property of hydraulic fluid used in grinding machine?

A] it must not control or absorb air

B] it must not cause corrosion of the moving parts

C] Should have adequate viscosity

D] it must vaporize at the operating temperature

119] Which one of the following is the advantage of pneumatic system?

A] For low cost layout

B] For increasing the rate of production

C] For better working environment

120] Following which advantage of Pneumatic power system

A] For increase production rate.

B] Less cash for layout

C] Good climate for work

D] Above all

121]The pressure of fluid in hydraulic brake system is governed by

A] boils law

B] Charles law

C] Pascal's law

D] none of the above laws

122] Allows fluid both way in and out of cylinder

A] Piston

B] Push Rod

C] Primary cup

D] Check valve

123] Relieves excess pressure of air from the air tank]

A] Air compressor

B] Unloader valve

C] Safety valve

D] Brake chamber

124] Regulates maximum air pressure, reaching to air tank]

A] Air compressor

B] Unloader valve

C] Safety valve

D] Brake chamber

125] Distributes air to various circuits

A] Brake actuator

B] Dual brake valve

C] System protection valve

126] A voltage source produces an IR drop of 40V across a 20 ohms resistance, 60V across a 30 ohms resistance and 180V across a 90 ohms resistance all in series]How much is the applied voltage?

A] 180 V

B] 240 V

C] 100 V

D] 280 V

127] The initial function of a choke in a tube light circuit is to...

A] limit the starting current

B] induce high voltage

C] heat up the filament

D] limit the current after starting

128] The peak-to-peak voltage is 99V]how big is the effective value of the sine wave?

A] 70 V

B] 44.5V

C] 49.5 V

D] 35 V

129]A moving coil voltmeter reads 10 V AC]How big is the effective voltage?

A] higher

B] lower

C] the same

D]10% higher

130]A capacitor is connected across a 200 volt AC line, its minimum voltage rating should be...

A]100 volts

B] 200 Volts

C]300 volts

D]400 volts

131]How much is the nominal output voltage of a carbon zinc cell?

A]12V

B]1.5V

C]2.0V

D]2.2V

132]Cells are connected in series to..

A]increase the output voltage

B]decreases the output voltage

C]decrease the internal resistance

D]increase the current capacity

133] An unknown DC voltage is to be measured, which measuring range will you select first?

A]500V

B]50V

C]1.5 V

D]0.5V

134]Heat developed in a conductor is proportional to the...

A]square of the power

B]square of the resistance

C]square of the current

D]square of the time

135]The second function of a choke in a tube light circuit is to...

A]limit the starting current

B]induce high voltage

C]heat up the filament

D]limit the current after starting

136]A moving iron ammeter reads 10 A]how big is the peak current of the oscillation?

A]7.07 A

B]1.1414A

C]70.7 A

D]14.1 A

137]Power companies are interested in improving the power factor to

A]reduce line current

B]increase motor efficiency

C]increase volt-amperes

D]decrease power

138] In a RL parallel circuit, the opposition to total current is called...
A]reactance
B]resistance
C]a vector sum
D]impedance
139] An unknown direct current of micro ampere rating is to be measured, which measuring range will you select first?
A]20 micro amp
B]15 micro amp
C]150 micro amp
D]500 micro amp
140]The earth conductor provides a path to ground for..
A] leakage current
B]over current
C]high voltage
D]circuit current
141]Which appliance works on heating effect of electric current?
A]incandescent lamp
B]bimetallic thermostat
C]H R C fuse
D]toaster
142] connect two terminals of solenoid]
A] Pinion
B] Over running clutch
C] Plunger disk
D] Clutch
143] When the horn button is pressed the current flows to horn through
A] Horn switch
B] Solenoid coil
C] Battery
D] Chassis]
144] Turns core to magnet
A] Solenoid Switch
B] Actuating wire (when heated]
C] Ballast Resistors
D] Actuating wire (when cooled]
145]A capacitor increases the power factor value of an AC motor load when it is connected...

A] in series with the motor

B]in series with the starter

C]in parallel with the motor

D]in series with the main winding

146]Synchronous motor when used for power factor improvement should be...

A]under excited

B]over excited

C]loaded

D]running at no load

147]If a winding makes electrical contact with the metal case of the mixer motor the winding is...

A]grounded

B]open circuited

C]short circuited

D]loose connected

148]If the end shafts of a rotor turns blue it is an indication of...

A]scoring

B]overheating

C]freezing

D]burring

149] Extreme pressure additive (EPA] is mixed with cutting fluid for improving its power of.

A] Cooling

B] Lubrication

D] Production of the machined surface

C] Cleaning of cutting zone

150] The main purpose for using a lubricant in machine tools is to ------

A] Cool down the making parts

B] Prevent machine tool from heating

C] Wet the making parts for close contact

D] Minimize the friction between the making parts

151] Preventive maintenance is ....]

A] The maintenance involves the use of sensitive instruments

B] The maintenance generally performed by operator himself

C] The work carried only when machine break down

D] plan to minimize the unforeseen break down

152] What is a break down maintenance?

A] Maintenance to minimize the unforeseen breakdown

B] Maintenance generally performed by operator himself

C] Maintenance involves replacement of worn out parts

D] Repairs work carried only when machine breakdown

153] The Routine Maintenance is ---------

A] it is planned maintenance to minimize the unforeseen breakdown

B] This type of maintenance involves the use of sensitive instrument

C] It is repair work carried only when machine breakdowns

D] This types of maintenance is generally performed by operator himself

154] The cutting edge of a solid tool is made of

A] carbon steel

B] mild steel

C] super high speed steel

D] stelite

155] The tip of a cemented carbide threading tool is

A] brazed

B] welded

C] soldered

D] clamped to the shank

156] Tool will rub against the work surfaces and the cutting force increases when..

A] The clearance angle is more

B] The clearance angel is less

C] The rake angle is more

D] The rake angle is less

157] Formation of a chip while cutting is based on the...

A] Rake angle of the tool

B] Clearance angle of the tool

C] Wedge angle of the tool

D] Clearance and wedge angle of the tool

158] in following drawing, which of the front clearance angel?

A] Front clearance angle

B] Wedge angle

C] Cutting angle

D] Back rake angle

159] When cutting tool start his action & cutting force in increase at this position subsequent effect of tool is..?

A] Clearance angle of tool is high

B] Clearance angle of tool is low

C] Rake angle of tool is low

D] Rake angle of tool is high

160] The purpose of Rake angle for tool is?

A] Right direction for mental chips

B] Good finishing on job

C] For increase life of tool

D] For avoid friction in between job & tool

161] The purpose of provide clearance angle for cutting tool is?

A] For right direction of metal cutting chips

B] reduce friction on hit of job

C] for sage of job friction

D] for better finishing on job

162] If cutting tools setting upper centre height done what happen?

A] Encrease top Rake angle

B] less top Rake angle

C] No effect on Top Rake angle

D] Encrease clearance angle

163] What happen if cutting tool setting done lower of center height?

A] Encrease top Rake angle

B] Decrease top Rake angle

C] No any effect on to Rake

D] Decrease clearance angle

164] If cutting tool is upsetting of centre of job?

A] Encrease front clearance angle

B] Decrease front clearance angle

C] no any effect on front clearance angle

D] none of them

165] If cutting tool is down setting of centre of job?

A] Front clearance angle is increase

B] Front clearance angle is decrease

C] No any effect on clearance angle

D] None of them

166] Zero Rake angle give for tool?

A] To avoid friction of tool

B] For increase tool life

C] For increase straight of tool

D] For better finishing on job

167] For carbide tip tool turning on hard material it has......essential?

A] Side Rake angle

B] Zero Rake angle

C] Positive Rake angle

D] Negative Rake angle

168] For do not break cutting edge of cutting tool...?

A] Feed increase

B] Cutting speed done low

C] Length of nose decrease

D] Use negative rake angle

169] Hydraulic energy is converted into another form of energy by hydraulic machines. What form of energy is that?

a) Mechanical Energy

b) Electrical Energy

c) Nuclear Energy

d) Elastic Energy

170] which principle is used in Hydraulic Turbines?

a) Faraday law

b) Newton's second law

c) Charles law

d) Braggs law

171] Buckets and blades used in a turbine are used to:

a) Alter the direction of water

b) Switch off the turbine

c) To regulate the wind speed

d) To regenerate the power

172] _______________is the electric power obtained from the energy of the water.

a) Roto dynamic power

b) Thermal power

c) Nuclear power

d) Hydroelectric power

173] Which energy generated in a turbine is used to run electric power generator linked to the turbine shaft?

a) Mechanical Energy

b) Potential Energy

c) Elastic Energy

d) Kinetic Energy

174] Hydraulic Machines fall under the category :

a) Pulverizers

b) Kinetic machinery

c) Condensers

d) Roto-dynamic machinery

175] Which kind of turbines changes the pressure of the water entered through it?

A) Reaction turbines

b) Impulse turbines

c) Reactive turbines

d) Kinetic turbines

176] Which type of turbine is used to change the velocity of the water through its flow?

a) Kinetic turbines

b) Axial flow turbines

c) Impulse turbines

d) Reaction turbines

177] Which type of turbine is a Francis Turbine?

a) Impulse Turbine

b) Screw Turbine

c) Reaction turbine

d) Turgo turbine

178]How many types of Reaction turbines are there?

a) 5

b) 4

c) 3

d) 9

179] Which kind of turbine is a Fourneyron Turbine?

a) Inward flow turbine

b) Outward flow turbine

c) Mixed flow turbine

d) Radial flow turbine

180] Fluid power circuits use schematic drawings to:

a) Simplify component function details

b) Make it so only trained persons can understand the functions

c) Make the drawing look impressive

d) Make untrained person to understand

181] A pneumatic symbol is:

a) Different from a hydraulic symbol used for the same function

b) The same as a hydraulic symbol used for the same function

c) Not to be compared to a hydraulic symbol used for the same function

d) None of the mentioned

182] Pneumatic systems usually do not exceed:

a) 1 hp

b) 1 to 2 hp

c) 2 to 3 hp

d) 4 to 5 hp

183] Most hydraulic circuits:

a) Operate from a central hydraulic power unit

b) Use air-over-oil power units

c) Have a dedicated power unit

d) Does not have dedicated power unit

184] Hydraulic and pneumatic circuits:

a) Perform the same way for all functions

b) Perform differently for all functions

c) Perform the same with some exceptions

d) Does not perform all the functions

185] The lubricator in a pneumatic circuit is the:

a) First element in line

b) Second element in line

c) Last element in line

d) Third element in line

186] When comparing first cost of hydraulic systems to pneumatic systems, generally they are:

a) More expensive to purchase

b) Less expensive to purchase

c) Cost is same

d) Cost is not required

187] When comparing operating cost of hydraulic systems to pneumatic systems, generally they are.

a) More expensive to operate

b) Less expensive to operate

c) Cost is same to operate

d) Cost is not required

188] The most common hydraulic fluid is:

a) Mineral oil

b) Synthetic fluid

c) Water

d) Gel

189) Which fluid is used in hydraulic power systems?

a] water

b] oil

c] non-compressible fluid

d] all of the above

190) Pressure of 1 bar is equal to

a] 14]5 psi

b] 145 psi

c] 12]5 psi

d] 145 x 10-6 psi

191) What effect does overloading have on fluid power and electrical systems?

a] electrical components get damaged in electrical systems

b] fluid power system stops working without damaging the components

c] both a] and b]

d] none of the above

192) How is power transmitted in fluid power systems?

a] power is transmitted instantaneously

b] power is transmitted gradually

c] both a] and b]

d] none of the above

193) Generally liquids are non-compressible but when a large pressure of 70 bar is applied, petroleum oil can be compressed up to

a] 0]5% of its original volume

b] 1% of its original volume

c] 5% of its original volume

d] none of the above

194) The resistance offered to the flow of fluid inside a piston develops into

a] pressure

b] force

c] stress

d] all of the above

195) At low pressures, liquids are

a] compressible

b] non-compressible

c] unpredictable

196) In hydraulic systems,

a] the mechanical energy is transferred to the oil and then converted into mechanical energy

b] the electrical energy is transferred to the oil and then converted into mechanical energy

c] the mechanical energy is transferred to the oil and converted into electrical energy

d] none of the above

197) Which of the following is used as a component in hydraulic power unit?

a] pressure gauge

b] filler gauge

c] valve

d] reservoir

198) Rotary motion in a hydraulic power unit is achieved by using

a] hydraulic cylinder

b] pneumatic cylinder

c] both hydraulic and pneumatic cylinder

d] none of the above

199) What is the relation between speed and flow rate for fixed displacement vane pump?

a] flow rate increases with increase in speed of rotor

b] flow rate decreases with increase in speed of rotor

c] flow rate is constant and does not change with change in speed

d] none of the above

200) In fixed displacement vane pump,

a] flow rate decreases with increase in working pressure

b] flow rate increases with increase in working pressure

c] flow rate is constant and does not change with working pressure

d] none of the above

201) Which type of motion is transmitted by hydraulic actuators?

a] linear motion

b] rotary motion

c] both a] and b]

d] none of the above

202) What is the function of electric actuator?

a] converts electrical energy into mechanical torque
b] converts mechanical torque into electrical energy
c] converts mechanical energy into mechanical torque
d] none of the above

203) Which of the following is a hydraulic cylinder based on construction?
a] single acting cylinder
b] double acting cylinder
c] welded design cylinder
d] all of the above

204) Which energy is converted into mechanical energy by the hydraulic cylinders?
a] hydrostatic energy
b] hydrodynamic energy
c] electrical energy
d] none of the above

205) What is the advantage of using a single acting cylinder?
a] high cost and reliable
b] honing inside the inner surface of pump is not required
c] piston seals are not required
d] all of the above

206) What is the function of a flow control valve?
a] flow control valve changes the direction of oil flow
b] flow control valve can adjust the flow rate of hydraulic oil
c] both a] and b]
d] none of the above

207) What does the numbers in 4/2 valve mean?
a] 4 positions and 2 ways
b] 4 ways and 2 positions
c] none of the above
d] 3 ways 2 positions

208) Which type of solenoid has more chances of coil failure?
a] AC solenoid
b] DC solenoid
c] both AC and DC solenoids
d] none of the above

209) Which stage in two stage direction control valve is solenoid operated?

a] main stage direction control valve
b] pilot stage direction control valve
c] both stages in two stage direction control are solenoid operated
d] none of the above

210) Which of the following is a gas charged accumulator?
a] bladder type
b] spring loaded accumulator
c] weighted accumulator
d] all of the above

211) How is pressure of fluid under piston calculated in a weighted accumulator?
a] pressure of fluid = (weight added / piston area)
b] pressure of fluid = (piston area / weight added)
c] pressure of fluid = (weight added / piston force)
d] pressure of fluid = (piston force / weight added)

212) Which of the following gas is used in gas charged accumulator?
a] oxygen
b] nitrogen
c] carbon dioxide
d] all of the above

213) The relation for rapid change in pressure and volume adiabatically is given as
a] p0 v0 = p1 v1 = p2 v2
b] p0 v0 = p1 v1n = p2 v2n
c] p0 v0n = p1 v1n = p2 v2n
d] none of the above

214) Why is the pilot operated check valve used in clamping operation?
a] to reduce leakage in spool valve
b] to avoid decrease in pressure during clamping
c] *both a] and b]*
d] none of the above

215) Which area does the part shown below indicate?
a] rod area
b] full bore area
c] annulus area
d] none of the above

216) Which of the following statements is true?
a] Meter-in feed circuits have speed control in two directions

b] Standard block feed circuits have speed control in two directions

c] Tank line feed control systems have speed control only in one direction

d] all of the above

217) Leakage in rotary chucks can be compensated by

a] flow control valve

b] pilot operated check valve

c] accumulator

d] all of the above

218) Which valve is used to block the accumulator from the system for the purpose of safety?

a] pilot valve

b] needle valve

c] detent valve

d] all of the above

219) Which of the following systems generate more energy when used in industrial applications?

a] hydraulic systems

b] pneumatic systems

c] both systems generate same energy

d] cannot say

220) Which type of compressor requires a reservoir for compressed air and why?

a] rotary compressor to avoid pulsating effect

b] reciprocating compressor to avoid pulsating effect

c] both rotary and reciprocating compressors to avoid pulsating effect

d] none of the above

221) Which of the following factors is/are considered while selecting a compressor?

a] type of oil filter required

b] volumetric efficiency

c] viscosity of the liquids used

d] all of the above

222) Which of the following is a component used in air generation system?

a] pressure switch

b] pressure gauge

c] drier

d] intercooler

223) Where is an intercooler connected in a two stage compressor?

a] intercooler is connected after the two stage compressor

b] intercooler is connected between the two stages of the compressor

c] intercooler is connected before the two stage compressor

d] none of the above

224) Which of the following notations is used to represent a regulator unit?

a] 3]0

b] 0]3

c] 3

d] none of the above

225) Which of the following logic valve is known as shuttle valve?

a] OR gate

b] AND gate

c] NOR gate

d] NAND

226) In pneumatic systems, AND gate is also known as

a] check valve

b] shuttle valve

c] dual pressure valve

d] none of the above

227) What is a pressure sequence valve?

a] it is a combination of adjustable pressure relief valve and directional control valve

b] it is a combination of nonadjustable pressure relief valve and directional control valve

c] it is a combination of adjustable pressure reducing valve and check valve

d] it is a combination of adjustable pressure reducing valve and flow control valve

228) Overlapping of signals in pneumatic systems can be avoided by using

a] rolling lever valve

b] idle roller lever valve

c] both a] and b]

d] none of the above

229) Which of the following statements is true for cascade method which is used to draw a pneumatic circuit?

a] signal processing valves are connected in parallel

b] when the number of signal processing valves are greater than 4, the signals are strong

c] cascade method does not consider the cost factor

d] all of the above

230) What is the part, shown in below diagram of 3/2 valve, called?

a] manually operated valve

b] pilot operated valve

c] pressure electric converter

d] none of the above

231) In which systems, spool of the servo valve is operated by a torque motor?

a] hydromechanical servo systems

b] electrohydraulic servo systems

c] conventional servo valve

d] all of the above

232) What does servo mean in servo valve system?

a] it cannot receive a feedback but the desired output can be obtained

b] it cannot receive a feedback and the desired output cannot be obtained

c] it can receive a feedback and the desired output can be obtained

d] none of the above

233) In conventional valves, which component is used to move the spool?

a] torque motor

b] mechanical servo valve

c] solenoid

d] all of the above

234) What is the advantage of DC solenoid coils?

a] DC solenoid coils have high rush in current

b] DC solenoid coils have constant level of current

c] DC solenoid coils have rating of 220 V DC

d] all of the above

235) Which of the following statements is true for a proportional valve?

a] spool of the proportional valve can travel maximum length

b] digital type of functioning is possible in proportional valve c] proportional valve requires a separate flow control valve

d] all of the above

236) Which of the following statements is/are false?

a] air is non-compressible

b] less power is developed in fluid power systems than conventional systems

c] mechanical linkages used for load handling purposes have high efficiency

d] <u>all of the above</u>

237) The hydraulic system is

a] less precise than pneumatic system

b] <u>more precise than pneumatic system</u>

c] both hydraulic and pneumatic systems are same on basis of precision

d] none of the above

238) Which energy is used to transmit power in hydrostatic system?

a] <u>pressure energy</u>

b] kinetic energy

c] potential energy

d] all of the above

239) Which system uses kinetic energy to transmit power?

a] hydrostatic system

b] <u>hydrodynamic system</u>

c] pneumatic system

d] none of the above

240) If no load is attached to piston rod, the movement of piston assembly is possible when

a] oil overcomes its self weight

b] oil overcomes friction in the piston rod assembly

c] <u>both a] and b]</u>

d] none of the above

241) Which factor helps in obtaining high speed of the piston rod in the hydraulic system?

a] decreased friction

b] pump capacity

c] increased flow rate

d] <u>all of the above</u>

242) During any operation in hydraulic system, oil prefers the path of

a] <u>least resistance</u>

b] maximum resistance

c] both a] and b]

d] none of the above

243) In a hydraulic circuit a pump is provided with two outlet paths, one where load is attached and other to the reservoir] Which path will the oil choose to flow first?

a] oil will flow to the path where load is attached

b] oil will flow back to the reservoir first

c] oil will flow through both the paths simultaneously

d] none of the above

244) Which of the following is used as an accessory in hydraulic power unit?

a] pumps

b] valves

c] motor

d] reservoir

245) Which type of pump is used for lifting water from the ground surface to the top of the building?

a] centrifugal pump

b] turbine pump

c] submersible pump

d] all of the above

246) Pumps used in hydraulic applications are

a] positive displacement pumps

b] variable displacement pumps

c] fixed displacement pumps

d] all of the above

247) What is a positive displacement pump?

a] oil from suction side of the pump flows completely to the delivery side

b] volume of fluid discharged cannot return back to the suction side of the pump

c] discharges fixed volume of fluid every cycle

d] all of the above

248) While operating a positive displacement pump,

a] the shut-off valve should be closed on delivery side

b] the shut-off valve should be closed on suction side

c] the shut-off valve should be opened on delivery side

d] none of the above

249) What effect does working pressure have on input power for radial piston pumps?

a] as working pressure increases input power decreases

b] as working pressure increases input power increases

c] pressure remains constant for different input powers

d] none of the above

250) Radial piston pumps can have,

a] cylinder block rotating and cam stationary

b] cylinder block stationary and cam rotating

c] both a] and b]

d] none of the above

251) Why are hydraulic cylinders cushioned?

a] cushioning decelerates the piston of a cylinder

b] stress and vibrations can be reduced

c] both a] and b]

d] none of the above

252) Which of the following statements is true?

a] Tie-rod cylinders are used in applications having working pressure of 70 bar

b] Welded type cylinders are used in systems having working pressure more than 70 bar

c] Tie-rod cylinders can be used in systems having working pressure more than 70 bar

d] all of the above

253) Which of these actions does a hydraulic cylinder perform?

a] pushing

b] lifting

c] both a] and b]

d] none of the above

254) Leakage in welded type of hydraulic cylinder is prevented by

a] wiper in gland cover

b] rod seal in end cover

c] rod seal in gland cover

d] none of the above

255)In single acting hydraulic cylinders the piston comes back to its original position due to

a] spring force

b] self-weight

c] momentum of a flywheel
d] all of the above
256) Check valve is a type of
a] pressure reducing valve
b] pressure relief valve
c] directional control valve
d] none of the above
257) A pressure relief valve can be
a] direct operated
b] pilot operated
c] solenoid operated
d] all of the above
258) How is reverse flow possible in pilot operated check valve?
a] spring force lifts the ball due to which reverse flow is possible
b] fluid pressure lifts the ball due to which reverse flow is possible
c] both a] and b]
d] none of the above
259) What is the difference between pressure relief valve and pressure reducing valve?
a] pressure reducing valve is connected between pump and tank line while pressure relief valve is connected between DCV and branch circuit
b] pressure relief valve is always normally opened
c] pressure reducing valve is connected between DCV and branch circuit while pressure relief valve is connected between pump and tank
d] none of the above
260) Accumulator used in gas charged accumulator is
a] hydraulic
b] pneumatic
c] hydropneumatic
d] none of the above
261) What is the function of pressure switch?
a] pressure switch is used to start a motor
b] pressure switch is used to stop a motor
c] pressure switch is used to de-energize a solenoid
d] all of the above
262) Intensifier used in pneumatic systems has output pressure
a] less than input pressure
b] more than input pressure

c] same as input pressure

d] none of the above

263) What is the function of unloading relief valve and can it be used as an accessory for accumulators?

a] unloading relief valve is used to charge the accumulator by a pump when accumulator pressure falls below the set value and it can be used as an accessory]

b] unloading relief valve is used to charge the accumulator by a pump when accumulator pressure falls below the set value but is not used as an accessory

c] unloading relief valve is used to charge the accumulator by a pump when accumulator pressure rises above the set value but is not used as an accessory

d] unloading relief valve is used to charge the accumulator by a pump when accumulator pressure rises above the set value and is used as an accessory

264) Cylinder has a bore area of 300 cm 2 and velocity of 180 cm/min] Calculate the flow rate of a pump

a] 55 l/min

b] 50 l/min

c] 54 l/min

d] none of the above

265) Which of the following statements is true, for two pumps used in circuit when initially fast operation is performed to reach a job and feeding operation is done at a slow speed?

a] initially to reach a job, a tool must be connected to a pump of high discharge and low pressure

b] initially to reach a job, a tool must be connected to a pump of low discharge and high pressure

c] for feeding operation low discharge low pressure pump is required

d] none of the above

266) What are different operations performed by PLC's?

a] Boolean logic

b] Timing

c] Arithmetic

d] all of the above

267) Which of the following pumps saves more power?

a] single pump

b] double pump

c] single and double pump use same amount of power

d] none of the above

268) What is the advantage of PLC?

a] easy to find errors

b] replacements can be easily made

c] PLC's are easily programmed

d] all of the above

269) Mass of water vapour in unit volume of air is known as

a] relative humidity

b] absolute humidity

c] saturation quantity

d] none of the above

270) Which valve is also known as memory valve?

a] single pilot signal valve

b] double pilot signal valve

c] roller lever valve

d] logic valve

271) What is the difference between signal air and control air?

a] signal air actuates final control valve and control air flows to the cylinder through the final control valve for forward and backward movement of piston rod

b] control air actuates final control valve and signal air flows to the cylinder through the final control valve for forward and backward movement of piston rod

c] both a] and b]

d] none of the above

272) Which of the following is used to sense the initial and final positions of a piston rod?

a] lever operated direction control valve

b] limit switch

c] roller lever valve

d] all of the above

273) Which valve gets activated only in one direction that is forward or backward movement of the piston rod?

a] roller lever valve

b] idle roller lever valve

c] both a] and b]

d] none of the above

274) Which numbers are used to denote retraction of a piston rod?

a] even numbers

b] odd numbers

c] both even and odd numbers

d] none of the above

275) Which of the following is an element of time delay valve?

a] flow control valve

b] direction control valve

c] both a] and b] d] none of the above

d] none of above

276) Which of the following is a type of cushioning in hydraulic cylinders?

a] trunnion cushioning

b] adjustable cushioning

c] clevis cushioning

d] none of the above

277) How is proximity switch differentiated from limit switch?

a] proximity switch is activated when moving parts have physical contact with it

b] proximity switch is activated when non-moving parts have physical contact

c] proximity switch is activated when moving parts are close to it

d] none of the above

278) Which of the following statements is true?

a] electromagnetic relays have high reliability at more cost

b] electromagnetic relays use low current and voltage, to have open or close contact in high voltage and current circuit

c] air pressure passed to pressure electric converter opens a contact which energizes a circuit for the flow of electric contact

d] all of the above

279) In which circuits, relay of low voltage and low current is used to make open or close contact?

a] high voltage and high current circuit

b] low voltage and low current circuit

c] high voltage and low current circuit

d] low voltage and low current circuit

280) In electropneumatic circuits,

a] spool is shifted by signal air
b] spool is shifted by control air
c] spool is shifted by electromotive force
d] all of the above

281) Why are electromechanical relays more popular than solid state relays?
a] they are reliable
b] less costly
c] both a] and b]
d] none of the above

282) In which control valve energy consumption reduces as load decreases?
a] conventional direction control valve
b] proportional direction control valve
c] both a] and b]
d] none of the above

283) Which of the following is a characteristic of servo valve?
a] open loop system
b] closed loop system
c] less contamination
d] all of the above

284) What is PLC?
a] Process logic control
b] Programmable language converter
c] Programmable logic control
d] Programmable logic converter

285) What causes burning of AC solenoid coil?
a] holding current
b] in rush current
c] current clamps
d] all of the above

286) When PLC connections are used instead of electrical connections, the order of operations to be performed can be interchanged by
a] changing hardwired connections
b] changing sequence of program
c] both a] and b]
d] none of the above

287) The heat generated in hydraulic systems can be absorbed by

a] lubrication

b] cooling

c] sealing

d] all of the above

288) For which of the following purpose hydraulic film acts as a seal between the machined cavity and spool?

a] to reduce leakage

b] for cooling purposes

c] for lubrication purposes

d] all of the above

289) Pressure applied on a fluid in a container is equally distributed in all directions and acts with

a] equal force on equal areas parallelly

b] equal force on different areas and at right angles

c] equal force on equal areas and at right angles

d] none of the above

290) Which law explains the behavior of hydraulic fluids under pressure?

a] Charles's law

b] Newtons law

c] Pascal's law

d] none of the above

291) Flow of oil in a pipe takes place due to

a] balanced forces

b] unbalanced forces

c] both balanced and unbalanced forces

d] none of the above

292) Pressure drop in pipes, occurs due to

a] frictional resistance

b] load

c] flow pattern

d] none of the above

293) How is laminar flow characterized in a straight pipe?

a] flow of high shear stress

b] flow of high velocity

c] flow of low-velocity

d] none of the above

294) Positive displacement pump used in hydraulic systems have

a] high viscosity of fluids
b] low efficiency
c] required volume of fluid cannot be discharged
d] all of the above

295) Electric motor has a speed of 1200 rpm and output rate of pump is 6 cc/rev] Calculate flow rate of pump in l/min
a] 6 l/min
b] 7]2 l/min
c] 5 l/min
d] none of the above

296) Calculate the power absorbed by the pump if, it has a flow rate of 20 cc/rev and develops a maximum pressure of 70 bar, when electric motor runs at a speed of 1200 rpm]
a] 1]9 kW
b] 2]8 kW
c] 2]3 kW
d] none of the above

297) Volumetric efficiency is the ratio of
a] theoretical flow rate to actual flow rate
b] actual flow rate to theoretical flow rate
c] actual fluid power to pump input power
d] none of the above

298) Which of the following is a hydrodynamic pump?
a] vane pump
b] centrifugal pump
c] gear pump
d] piston pump

299) What causes reduction in speed of the piston rod when the hydraulic cylinder is cushioned?
a] oil flow through small space
b] back pressure created in the system
c] both a] and b
d] none of the above

300) Which of the following is a hydraulic cylinder based on application?
a] welded
b] bolted
c] ram
d] all of the above

301) What happens when supply of oil to a single acting cylinder is stopped?

a] no pressure is exerted on the system

b] more pressure is exerted on the piston

c] less pressure is exerted on the piston

d] none of the above

302) When does expansion of spring and retraction of cylinder take place in spring type single acting cylinder?

a] oil pressure exerted is less than spring compression pressure

b] oil pressure exerted is more than spring compression pressure

c] oil pressure exerted and spring compression pressure are same

d] none of the above

303) In a telescopic cylinder, as the number of stages increase

a] diameter of piston rod also increases

b] diameter of piston rod decreases

c] diameter of the piston rod remains the same

d] none of the above

304) Why are bleed off circuits used?

a] bleed off circuit is used to restrict the flow of fluid into the hydraulic cylinder

b] bleed off circuit is used to restrict the flow of fluid out of the hydraulic cylinder

c] bleed off circuits are used to reduce the speed of actuator

d] all of the above

305) Which of the following is applicable for bleed off circuits?

a] bleed off circuits develop heat in the system

b] bleed off circuits are used for resistive loads

c] bleed off circuits are used for runaway loads

d] all of the above

306) What is the function of sequence valve used in hydraulic circuits?

a] sequence valves are used to perform number of operations one after the other after the set pressure is reached

b] sequence valves are used to perform number of operations continuously before the set pressure is reached

c] sequence valves after reaching set pressure oil is flown to the tank

d] all of the above

307) When is a pressure reducing valve used?

a] it is used when higher pressure than system pressure is required

b] it is used when lower pressure than system pressure is required
c] when absolutely zero pressure is required
d] all of the above

308) How is strong magnetic field in a solenoid achieved?
a] strong magnetic field in a solenoid is achieved, if coil acts as conductor
b] coil is surrounded by a iron frame
c] iron core is placed at the centre of the coil
d] all of the above

309) What is the DC range of of solenoids in pneumatic systems?
a] 12 V and 24 V
b] 110 V and 220 V
c] both a] and b]
d] none of the above

310) Which of the following is used an output device on a ladder diagram?
a] proximity sensor
b] detent switch
c] relay
d] all of the above

311) The output device on a ladder diagram is represented by
a] square
b] circle
c] rectangle
d] semicircle

312) In mnemonics instructions, what does I in LDI indicate?
a] switch is normally open
b] switch is normally closed
c] it indicates operating of second switch
d] none of the above

313) In industrial applications hydraulic fluids have viscosity grade ranging from
a] 20 to 50
b] 70 to 95
c] 46 to 68
d] 15 to 44

314) High viscosity fluids have
a] low pressure drop
b] less power consumption

c] slow operation

d] all of the above

315) What is viscosity index?

a] effect of pressure on changes in viscosity

b] effect of temperature on changes in viscosity

c] effect of resistance between two surfaces

d] none of the above

316) Which property decides the behavior of fluid when mixed with water?

a] pour point

b] demulsibility

c] viscosity

d] oxidation

317) For any operation in a hydraulic system the fluid should have pour point

a] 20 0F below the lowest temperature

b] 20 0F above the lowest temperature

c] 20 0C below the lowest temperature

d] 20 0C above the lowest temperature

318) What is the disadvantage of petroleum based fluids?

a] low flash point

b] low density

c] light weight

d] all of the above

319) How is the water content in High Water Fluids (HFA) compared to oil content?

a] more oil than water

b] oil and water are in same proportion

c] more water than oil

d] contains only water

320) A fluid used in hydraulic systems should have

a] low oxidation resistance

b] high oxidation resistance

c] high oxidation enhancing ability

d] none of the above

321) At which pressure, petroleum oil used in hydraulic systems gets compressed by 1/2%?

a] 70 bar

b] 40 bar

c] 30 bar

d] 95 bar

322) What is the relation between temperature and specific weight for water glycol?

a] as temperature increases specific weight decreases

b] as temperature increases specific weight increases

c] temperature and specific weight vary linearly

d] none of the above

323) What is the relation between temperature and viscosity for hydraulic oil?

a] temperature and viscosity vary linearly

b] as temperature decreases viscosity decreases at atmospheric pressure

c] as temperature increases viscosity decreases at atmospheric pressure

d] none of the above

324) High Water Fluids contain

a] oil in water

b] water in oil

c] only water

d] none of the above

325) Viscosity of High Water Fluid is

a] greater than water

b] less than water

c] nearby water

d] none of the above

326) Adding an additive to water glycol fluids improves

a] flammability

b] viscosity

c] oxidation

d] all of the above

327) What is the characteristic of turbulent flow?

a] high velocity

b] the direction of flow and movement of particles is same

c] change in cross section does not affect the flow

d] all of the above

328) Which flow pattern gets affected when cross section of the pipe is changed?

a] laminar flow

b] turbulent flow
c] laminar and turbulent
d] none of the above

329) Speed of the actuator is affected by
a] cross-section area of the orifice
b] velocity of flow
c] <u>pipe diameter</u>
d] all of the above

330) In which of these applications Bernoulli's principle is widely used?
a] design of blowers
b] <u>design of aircraft wings</u>
c] design of propellers
d] all of the above

331) The total energy developed by the hydraulic oil in a system is given as
a] Total energy = (Potential energy + Pressure energy)
b] Total energy = (Potential energy + Kinetic energy)
c] Total energy = (Potential energy – Kinetic energy)
d] <u>none of the above</u>

332) If a pump gives higher flow rate to the valve then, pressure drop in the valve
a] increases
b] <u>decreases</u>
c] remains the same
d] none of the above

333) In Reynolds number (?vd) / μ, the letter μ denotes
a] kinematic viscosity
b] <u>absolute viscosity</u>
c] coefficient of friction
d] none of the above

334) The ratio of inertia force to viscosity is known as
a] Biot number
b] <u>Reynold number</u>
c] Cauchy number
d] Euler number

335) The Reynolds number for laminar flow is
a] more than 2800
b] <u>more than 2000</u>

c] less than 2000

d] between 2000 and 2800]

336) A pipe has a diameter of 0]2 m in which a fluid flows with a velocity of 0]3 m3/s] Determine whether the flow is laminar or turbulent calculating the Reynolds number] Assume kinematic viscosity = 0]5 × 10-4 m2 /s]

a] the flow is laminar having Reynolds number 1200

b] the flow is turbulent having Reynolds number 2100

c] the flow is laminar having Reynolds number 2200

d] the flow is neither laminar nor turbulent

337) What is the advantage of internal gear pump?

a] moderate speed

b] medium pressure

c] high viscosity fluids can be used

d] all of the above

338) The rotation of which inner element causes the liquid to pump out in centrifugal pumps?

a] internal gear

b] rotation of the impeller

c] cylinder rotor

d] none of the above

339) Which force causes vanes to come out of the rotor slots?

a] centripetal force

b] centrifugal force

c] friction force

d] none of the above

340) Which of the following statements is true?

a] combination of stator with rotor is known as cartridge unit

b] combination of stator with vanes is known as cartridge unit

c] combination of rotor with vanes is known as cartridge unit

d] none of the above

341) What is the advantage of flexible vane pump?

a] they can handle solids which are of large size

b] they can create good vacuum

c] both a] and b]

d] none of the above

342) Cartridge kits generate pumping chambers of various sizes, which

a] increase the flow rate

b] decrease the flow rate

c] increase and decrease the flow rate

d] none of the above

343) Which of the following statements is false for vane pumps?

a] wear in contact surfaces occurs due to continuous contact between vane tips and the cam ring

b] different sizes of cartridge kits can be replaced in same vane pump

c] elliptical cam ring is replaced by round cam ring to reduce unbalanced forces

d] none of the above

344) Balanced vane pumps are designed to have

a] fixed displacement

b] variable displacement

c] both fixed and variable displacement

d] none of the above

345) Cam ring of unbalanced vane pump is

a] round

b] elliptical

c] both a] and b]

d] none of the above

346) Which type of displacement is observed in gear pumps?

a] only variable displacement

b] only fixed displacement

c] both fixed and variable displacement

d] none of the above

347) What is the principle of operation used in gear pumps?

a] two gears rotate in same direction

b] two gears rotate in opposite direction

c] both a] and b]

d] none of the above

348) What causes suction of fluid into the gear pump?

a] when pressure drops during disengagement of teeth at the suction side

b] when pressure increases during disengagement of teeth at the suction side

c] when pressure drops during engagement of teeth at the suction side

d] when pressure increases during engagement of teeth at the suction side

349) How is the smooth and continuous discharge of fluid achieved in a gear pump?

a] increasing number of teeth

b] decreasing number of teeth

c] none of the above

d] all of above

350) The rotation of gears in internal gear pump takes place in

a] same direction

b] different direction

c] none of the above

d] all of above

351) How does the fluid flow in internal gear pump?

a] fluid enters the suction side between rotor, which is a large exterior gear and idler which is a small interior gear

b] fluid enters the suction side between rotor, which is a small exterior gear and idler which is a large interior gear

c] fluid enters the suction side between rotor and idler which rotate in different directions

d] none of the above

352) What causes internal leakage in internal gear pump?

a] less tolerance level between the meshing surfaces

b] more tolerance level between the meshing surfaces

c] no tolerance between the meshing surfaces

d] none of the above

353) What is the relation between pressure and overall efficiency for a gear pump?

a] as pressure increases, overall efficiency decreases

b] as pressure increases, overall efficiency increases

c] overall efficiency is not affected by change in pressure

d] cannot say

354) Which of the following statements is true for standard hydraulic cylinder and a telescopic cylinder?

a] telescopic and standard cylinders give same stroke length

b] telescopic cylinders give lesser stroke length than standard cylinder

c] telescopic cylinders give greater stroke length than standard cylinder

d] none of the above

355) Telescopic cylinders have

a] only two stage units

b] only three stage units

c] two or three stage units

d] multistage units

356) Which type of hydraulic cylinder has one piston connected to piston rod extended on both the sides of the cylinder?

a] telescopic cylinder

b] tandem cylinder

c] both a] and b]

d] none of the above

357) Which factor decides the working pressure of a hydraulic cylinder?

a] diameter of circular flange

b] bore diameter of cylinder

c] stroke length

d] all of the above

358) Which factor is considered while selecting the diameter of piston rod in hydraulic cylinder?

a] bore diameter

b] length of stroke

c] load

d] all of the above

359) Which end of the hydraulic cylinder, the male clevis is mounted on?

a] cap end

b] rod end

c] both a] and b]

d] none of the above

360) Which of the following is used for mounting purpose in hydraulic cylinders?

a] Female clevis

b] Circular flange

c] Trunnion

d] all of the above

361) How does cushioning affect the speed of the piston when the cylinder is cushioned at extreme end?

a] cushioning decreases the speed of piston near the extreme ends of the cylinder

b] cushioning increases the speed of piston near the extreme ends of the cylinder c] cushioning increases the speed of piston at the beginning of the stroke in the cylinder

d] cushioning decreases the speed of piston at the beginning of the stroke in the cylinder

362) In adjustable type of cushioning,

a] piston rod can be moved at very slow speed

b] piston rod can be moved at increased speed

c] both a] and b]

d] none of the above

363) Which formula is used to calculate head loss in valves?

a] K2 (v / 2 g)

b] K (v / 2 g)

c] K (v2 / 2 g)

d] none of the above

364) What is the difference between vane pump and radial piston pump?

a] in radial piston pump, radial slots in vane pumps are replaced by radial bores which accommodate pistons

b] in radial piston pump, radial slots in vane pumps are replaced by radial bores which accommodate swash plate

c] in radial piston pump, radial slots in vane pumps are replaced by radial bores which accommodate both swash plate and pistons

d] none of the above

365) How many strokes does a single piston pump need to discharge oil?

a] one stroke

b] two strokes

c] three strokes

d] none of the above

366) How is the arrangement of pistons in piston pumps?

a] axially

b] radially

c] both a] and b]

d] none of the above

367) In which of these pumps, swash plate is used to translate the motion of rotating shaft into reciprocating motion?

a] radial piston pumps

b] axial piston pump

c] bent axis piston pump

d] all of the above

368) Which factors are considered while designing a axial piston pump?

a] use of swash plate

b] application in open loop or closed loop circuit

c] design of bent axis piston pump

d] all of the above

369) Angle of swash plate in axial piston pump is adjusted by

a] compensator

b] yoke

c] both a] and b]

d] none of the above

370) In axial piston pump, the yoke is pushed away from cylinder block due to which,

a] yoke angle increases

b] swash plate angle decreases

c] both a] and b]

d] none of the above

371) When the angle of swash plate decreases

a] flow rate increases

b] flow rate decreases

c] flow rate does not depend on swash plate angle

d] none of the above

372) What will be the discharge of oil in axial piston pump, when the angle of swash plate is zero?

a] discharge of oil is maximum

b] discharge of oil is minimum

c] there is no discharge of oil

d] none of the above

373) A bent axis piston pump has

a] pump axis bent

b] cylinder block which is inclined at an angle to the drive shaft

c] both a] and b]

d] none of the above

374) In which of these pumps, swash plate is replaced by cylinder block?

a] bent axis piston pump

b] radial piston pump

c] axial piston pump

d] none of the above

375) What happens when the distance between flange and cylinder block is varied?

a] piston displacement cannot be varied

b] variable flow rate of fluid can be achieved

c] fixed flow rate can be achieved

d] all of the above

376) What is the maximum angle between cylinder block and shaft axis?

a] 30o

b] 50o

c] 45o

d] all of the above

377) When does holding piston keep the angle between yoke and cylinder block maximum?

a] when set pressure is greater than load pressure

b] when set pressure is less than load pressure

c] when set pressure and load pressure are same

d] all of the above

378) Low-torque high-speed motors are used in

a] cranes

b] winches

c] fans

d] all of the above

379) Which motor causes heavy loads due to its usage in order to move at constant lower speeds?

a] Low-torque high-speed motors

b] High-torque low-speed motors

c] both a] and b]

d] none of the above

380) Motors used in high speed applications have

a] high torque with high speed

b] low torque with high speed

c] high torque with low speed

d] none of the above

381) Which of the following is a type of low-torque high-speed motor?

a] radial piston motors

b] axial piston motors

c] bent axis motor

d] gear motor

382) Cam lobe hydraulic motor is a type of

a] axial hydraulic motor

b] orbit hydraulic motor

c] gear hydraulic motor

d] radial hydraulic motor

INDUSTRIAL TRAINING INSTITUTE

Monthly Test-1, Marks- 20, Date:- _______________

(Every Question Carry Two Marks)

8] The metal for manufacturing jig bush is...?

A] mild steel

B] cast iron

C] cast steel

D] tool steel

9] Given following bush which busing used for locating renewable bushing?

A] press fit bushing

B] linear bushing

C] special bushing

D] knurd bushing

10] jig has tolerance..?

A] five present of job tolerance

B] ten percent of job tolerance

C] 20% to 50% of job tolerance

D] 100% of job tolerance

11] Following which jig is use for location from bore?

A] plate jig

B] solid jig

C] post jig

D] box jig

12] Following which jig having drill plate?

A] solid jig

B] plate jig

C] box jig

D] table jig

13] Following which locator is used for internal diameter location?

A] solid saports

B] Pin type locator

C] Vee locator

D] nest locator

14] Drm jig bushing-are generally hardened to ------------]

A] Mild steel

B] Cast iron

C] Cast steel

D] Tooi steel

15] Jigs is device which -------------

A] Locate the work piece

B] Holding and supporting the work piece

C] Guide the cutting tool

D] Does all the above

16] Which among the following jigs is used forllocation from a bore?

A] Plate jig

B] Solid jig

C] Post jig

D] Box jig

17] Fixture is a production device which -----------]

A] Holds and locate the work piece

B] Holds the piece

C] Chats the work piece,

D] Neither holds nor]Locates the-work piece

INDUSTRIAL TRAINING INSTITUTE

Monthly Test-2, Marks- 20, Date:- _______________

(Every Question Carry Two Marks)

18] Which one of the following is used to guide tool and hold the job in mass production? ‘

A] Gauge]

B] Housing

C] Fixture

D] Jig

19] Which among the following is the purpose for proi/iding bushing in a drill jig?

A] For locating accurately and guiding the drill for precise drilling operation

B] For determining the size of the hole to be drilled

C] For easy drilling

D] For getting good finished surface in the drilled holes

20] Drill jig are used for? _

A] Drill operations only]

B] Clamping the job for drilling

C] Drilling, Reaming, Tapping and other operations

D] Guiding the tools only

21] Which one of the following jigs consists of drill plate, which rests on the component to be

drilled?

A] Solid jig

B] Plate jig

C] Box jig

D] Trunnion jig

22] Jig is a device which -----------

A] Locates the work piece]

B] Hold and supports the work piece and guides tool

C] Guides the cutting tool

D] Hold the cutting tool]

23] Drill jig are used for ....]

A] Drilling, reaming, tapping and other allied operations

B] Drilling operations only

C] Clamping the job when drilling

D] Guiding the tool only

24] Fixture is a production device which---------: -----

A] holds the work piece '

B] Locate the work piece

C] Holds and locates the work piece

D] Neither holds nor locates the work piece

25] Purpose of the Box Jig is to

A] Hold the job and guide the tool to produce internal threads

B] To produce many inclined holes

C] To produce many straight holes

D] None of these

26] Jigs and fixtures are --------]

A] Machining tools

B] Precision tools

C] Both (a] & (b]

D] None of these

27] 'How jig are in terms of weight compared to fixtures?

A] Jigs are lighter than fixtures

B] Jigs are heavier than fixtures

C] jigs are equal in weight to fixtures for same operation

D] None of these

INDUSTRIAL TRAINING INSTITUTE

Monthly Test-3, Marks- 20, Date:- ______________

(Every Question Carry Two Marks)

28] Which fixtures are used for machining parts which musthav-e machined details evenw spaced?

A] Profile fixtures

B] Duplex fixtures

C] Indexing fixtures

D] None of these

29]What is the profile of the knife cutting edge of the upper blade of the hand level shear?

A] curved

B] straight

C] inclined

D] bevelled

105] In CNC program which miscellaneous function used for change of workpiece

A] M30

B] M60

C] M68

D] M78

106] The machine is.........for zero off-setting on CNC Machine.

A] In MDI Mode

B] In JOG Mode

C] In Automatic Mode

D] In Present Mode

107] The feed rate on NC Machine is indicate by ......code.

A] X

B] Y

C] F

D] Z

108] The position of axis is indicate by.......code.

A] X,Y,Z

B] P,Q,R

C] A,B,C

D] M,N,O

109] CNC Drilling Machine is on.......Axis Programmed.

A] Two Axis

B] Three Axis

C] Four Axis

D] Six Axis

110] From.......unit collect instruction in control unit of CNC

A] Machine Tool

B] Instruction

C] Magnetic Box

D] Memory

111] For preparing tape of NC Machine----------code is used.

A] EIA Code

B] ISO Code

C] ASC Code

D] None of them.

112] CNC Machine gives more accurate production than convention machine, But it is more

expensive because.

A] It has AC cabin

B] It has dust proof cabin

C] It has strong foundation

D] It has more space

INDUSTRIAL TRAINING INSTITUTE

Monthly Test-4, Marks- 20, Date:- _______________

(Every Question Carry Two Marks)

113] CNC Machine is working on graphical base the point on digital line, indicated digital points call..........

A] Graph

B] Input Media

C] Co-Ordinate

D] Original Point

114] On CNC Machine for longitudinal feed has.......axes, cross feed......axis and for vertical feed........axis name given.

A] A,B,C

B] X,Y,Z

C] P,Q,R

D] M,N,O

115] For rotary motion CNC machine axis has.......name given.

A] A,B,C

B] X,Y,Z

C] P,Q,R

D] M,N,O

116] CNC Machine means.......

A] Natural Control Machine

B] Pneumatic control Machine

C] Numerical Control Machine

D] No Command Machine

117] The inner formers of a hydraulic pipe bending machine are able to bend pipes up to a

diameter of

A] 40mm

B] 100mm

C] 20mm

D] 75mm

118] Which is not the property of hydraulic fluid used in grinding machine?

A] it must not control or absorb air

B] it must not cause corrosion of the moving parts

C] Should have adequate viscosity

D] it must vaporize at the operating temperature

119] Which one of the following is the advantage of pneumatic system?

A] For low cost layout

B] For increasing the rate of production

C] For better working environment

120] Following which advantage of Pneumatic power system

A] For increase production rate.

B] Less cash for layout

C] Good climate for work

D] Above all

121]The pressure of fluid in hydraulic brake system is governed by

A] boils law

B] Charles law

C] Pascal's law

D] none of the above laws

122] Allows fluid both way in and out of cylinder

A] Piston
B] Push Rod
C] Primary cup
D] Check valve

INDUSTRIAL TRAINING INSTITUTE
Monthly Test-5, Marks- 20, Date:- ______________
(Every Question Carry Two Marks)

123] Relieves excess pressure of air from the air tank]
A] Air compressor
B] Unloader valve
C] Safety valve
D] Brake chamber

124] Regulates maximum air pressure, reaching to air tank]
A] Air compressor
B] Unloader valve
C] Safety valve
D] Brake chamber

125] Distributes air to various circuits
A] Brake actuator
B] Dual brake valve
C] System protection valve

126] A voltage source produces an IR drop of 40V across a 20 ohms resistance, 60V across a 30 ohms resistance and 180V across a 90 ohms resistance all in series]How much is the applied voltage?
A] 180 V
B] 240 V
C] 100 V
D] 280 V

127] The initial function of a choke in a tube light circuit is to...
A] limit the starting current
B] induce high voltage
C] heat up the filament
D] limit the current after starting

128] The peak-to-peak voltage is 99V]how big is the effective value of the sine wave?
A] 70 V
B] 44.5V
C] 49.5 V

D] 35 V

129]A moving coil voltmeter reads 10 V AC]How big is the effective voltage?

A] higher

B] lower

C] the same

D]10% higher

130]A capacitor is connected across a 200 volt AC line, its minimum voltage rating should be...

A]100 volts

B] 200 Volts

C]300 volts

D]400 volts

131]How much is the nominal output voltage of a carbon zinc cell?

A]12V

B]1.5V

C]2.0V

D]2.2V

132]Cells are connected in series to..

A]increase the output voltage

B]decreases the output voltage

C]decrease the internal resistance

D]increase the current capacity

INDUSTRIAL TRAINING INSTITUTE

Monthly Test-6, Marks- 20, Date:- _______________

(Every Question Carry Two Marks)

133] An unknown DC voltage is to be measured, which measuring range will you select first?

A]500V

B]50V

C]1.5 V

D]0.5V

134]Heat developed in a conductor is proportional to the...

A]square of the power

B]square of the resistance

C]square of the current

D]square of the time

135]The second function of a choke in a tube light circuit is to...

A]limit the starting current

B]induce high voltage

C]heat up the filament

D]limit the current after starting

136]A moving iron ammeter reads 10 A]how big is the peak current of the oscillation?

A]7.07 A

B]1.1414A

C]70.7 A

D]14.1 A

137]Power companies are interested in improving the power factor to

A]reduce line current

B]increase motor efficiency

C]increase volt-amperes

D]decrease power

138] In a RL parallel circuit, the opposition to total current is called...

A]reactance

B]resistance

C]a vector sum

D]impedance

139] An unknown direct current of micro ampere rating is to be measured, which measuring range will you select first?

A]20 micro amp

B]15 micro amp

C]150 micro amp

D]500 micro amp

140]The earth conductor provides a path to ground for..

A] leakage current

B]over current

C]high voltage

D]circuit current

141]Which appliance works on heating effect of electric current?

A]incandescent lamp

B]bimetallic thermostat

C]H R C fuse

D]toaster

142] connect two terminals of solenoid]

A] Pinion

B] Over running clutch

C] Plunger disk

D] Clutch

INDUSTRIAL TRAINING INSTITUTE

Monthly Test-7, Marks- 20, Date:- ______________

(Every Question Carry Two Marks)

143] When the horn button is pressed the current flows to horn through

A] Horn switch

B] Solenoid coil

C] Battery

D] Chassis]

144] Turns core to magnet

A] Solenoid Switch

B] Actuating wire (when heated]

C] Ballast Resistors

D] Actuating wire (when cooled]

145]A capacitor increases the power factor value of an AC motor load when it is connected...

A] in series with the motor

B]in series with the starter

C]in parallel with the motor

D]in series with the main winding

146]Synchronous motor when used for power factor improvement should be...

A]under excited

B]over excited

C]loaded

D]running at no load

147]If a winding makes electrical contact with the metal case of the mixer motor the winding

is...

A]grounded

B]open circuited

C]short circuited

D]loose connected

148]If the end shafts of a rotor turns blue it is an indication of...

A]scoring

B]overheating

C]freezing

D]burring

149] Extreme pressure additive (EPA] is mixed with cutting fluid for improving its power of.

A] Cooling

B] Lubrication

D] Production of the machined surface

C] Cleaning of cutting zone

150] The main purpose for using a lubricant in machine tools is to ------

A] Cool down the making parts

B] Prevent machine tool from heating

C] Wet the making parts for close contact

D] Minimize the friction between the making parts

151] Preventive maintenance is ....]

A] The maintenance involves the use of sensitive instruments

B] The maintenance generally performed by operator himself

C] The work carried only when machine break down

D] plan to minimize the unforeseen break down

152] What is a break down maintenance?

A] Maintenance to minimize the unforeseen breakdown

B] Maintenance generally performed by operator himself

C] Maintenance involves replacement of worn out parts

D] Repairs work carried only when machine breakdown

INDUSTRIAL TRAINING INSTITUTE

Monthly Test-8, Marks- 20, Date:- ______________

(Every Question Carry Two Marks)

153] The Routine Maintenance is ---------

A] it is planned maintenance to minimize the unforeseen breakdown

B] This type of maintenance involves the use of sensitive instrument

C] It is repair work carried only when machine breakdowns

D] This types of maintenance is generally performed by operator himself

154] The cutting edge of a solid tool is made of

A] carbon steel

B] mild steel

C] super high speed steel

D] stelite

155] The tip of a cemented carbide threading tool is

A] brazed

B] welded

C] soldered

D] clamped to the shank

156] Tool will rub against the work surfaces and the cutting force increases when..

A] The clearance angle is more

B] The clearance angel is less

C] The rake angle is more

D] The rake angle is less

157] Formation of a chip while cutting is based on the...

A] Rake angle of the tool

B] Clearance angle of the tool

C] Wedge angle of the tool

D] Clearance and wedge angle of the tool

158] in following drawing, which of the front clearance angel?

A] Front clearance angle

B] Wedge angle

C] Cutting angle

D] Back rake angle

159] When cutting tool start his action & cutting force in increase at this position subsequent effect of tool is..?

A] Clearance angle of tool is high

B] Clearance angle of tool is low

C] Rake angle of tool is low

D] Rake angle of tool is high

160] The purpose of Rake angle for tool is?

A] Right direction for mental chips

B] Good finishing on job

C] For increase life of tool

D] For avoid friction in between job & tool

161] The purpose of provide clearance angle for cutting tool is?

A] For right direction of metal cutting chips

B] reduce friction on hit of job

C] for sage of job friction

D] for better finishing on job

162] If cutting tools setting upper centre height done what happen?

A] Encrease top Rake angle

B] less top Rake angle

C] No effect on Top Rake angle

D] Encrease clearance angle

INDUSTRIAL TRAINING INSTITUTE

Monthly Test-9, Marks- 20, Date:- ______________

(Every Question Carry Two Marks)

163] What happen if cutting tool setting done lower of center height?

A] Encrease top Rake angle

B] Decrease top Rake angle

C] No any effect on to Rake

D] Decrease clearance angle

164] If cutting tool is upsetting of centre of job?

A] Encrease front clearance angle

B] Decrease front clearance angle

C] no any effect on front clearance angle

D] none of them

165] If cutting tool is down setting of centre of job?

A] Front clearance angle is increase

B] Front clearance angle is decrease

C] No any effect on clearance angle

D] None of them

166] Zero Rake angle give for tool?

A] To avoid friction of tool

B] For increase tool life

C] For increase straight of tool

D] For better finishing on job

167] For carbide tip tool turning on hard material it has......essential?

A] Side Rake angle

B] Zero Rake angle

C] Positive Rake angle

D] Negative Rake angle

168] For do not break cutting edge of cutting tool...?

A] Feed increase

B] Cutting speed done low

C] Length of nose decrease

D] Use negative rake angle

169] Hydraulic energy is converted into another form of energy by hydraulic machines. What form of energy is that?

a) Mechanical Energy

b) Electrical Energy
c) Nuclear Energy
d) Elastic Energy

170] which principle is used in Hydraulic Turbines?
a) Faraday law
b) Newton's second law
c) Charles law
d) Braggs law

171] Buckets and blades used in a turbine are used to:
a) Alter the direction of water
b) Switch off the turbine
c) To regulate the wind speed
d) To regenerate the power

172] _______________is the electric power obtained from the energy of the water.
a) Roto dynamic power
b) Thermal power
c) Nuclear power
d) Hydroelectric power

INDUSTRIAL TRAINING INSTITUTE

Monthly Test-10, Marks- 20, Date:- _____________

(Every Question Carry Two Marks)

173] Which energy generated in a turbine is used to run electric power generator linked to the turbine shaft?
a) Mechanical Energy
b) Potential Energy
c) Elastic Energy
d) Kinetic Energy

174] Hydraulic Machines fall under the category :
a) Pulverizers
b) Kinetic machinery
c) Condensers
d) Roto-dynamic machinery

175] Which kind of turbines changes the pressure of the water entered through it?
A) Reaction turbines
b) Impulse turbines
c) Reactive turbines

d) Kinetic turbines

176] Which type of turbine is used to change the velocity of the water through its flow?

a) Kinetic turbines

b) Axial flow turbines

c) Impulse turbines

d) Reaction turbines

177] Which type of turbine is a Francis Turbine?

a) Impulse Turbine

b) Screw Turbine

c) Reaction turbine

d) Turgo turbine

178]How many types of Reaction turbines are there?

a) 5

b) 4

c) 3

d) 9

179] Which kind of turbine is a Fourneyron Turbine?

a) Inward flow turbine

b) Outward flow turbine

c) Mixed flow turbine

d) Radial flow turbine

180] Fluid power circuits use schematic drawings to:

a) Simplify component function details

b) Make it so only trained persons can understand the functions

c) Make the drawing look impressive

d) Make untrained person to understand

181] A pneumatic symbol is:

a) Different from a hydraulic symbol used for the same function

b) The same as a hydraulic symbol used for the same function

c) Not to be compared to a hydraulic symbol used for the same function

d) None of the mentioned

182] Pneumatic systems usually do not exceed:

a) 1 hp

b) 1 to 2 hp

c) 2 to 3 hp

d) 4 to 5 hp

Monthly Test-11, Marks- 20, Date:- ______________

(Every Question Carry Two Marks)

183] Most hydraulic circuits:

a) Operate from a central hydraulic power unit

b) Use air-over-oil power units

c) Have a dedicated power unit

d) Does not have dedicated power unit

184] Hydraulic and pneumatic circuits:

a) Perform the same way for all functions

b) Perform differently for all functions

c) Perform the same with some exceptions

d) Does not perform all the functions

185] The lubricator in a pneumatic circuit is the:

a) First element in line

b) Second element in line

c) Last element in line

d) Third element in line

186] When comparing first cost of hydraulic systems to pneumatic systems, generally they are:

a) More expensive to purchase

b) Less expensive to purchase

c) Cost is same

d) Cost is not required

187] When comparing operating cost of hydraulic systems to pneumatic systems, generally they

are.

a) More expensive to operate

b) Less expensive to operate

c) Cost is same to operate

d) Cost is not required

188] The most common hydraulic fluid is:

a) Mineral oil

b) Synthetic fluid

c) Water

d) Gel

189) Which fluid is used in hydraulic power systems?

a] water

b] oil

c] non-compressible fluid

d] all of the above

190) Pressure of 1 bar is equal to

a] 14]5 psi

b] 145 psi

c] 12]5 psi

d] 145 x 10-6 psi

191) What effect does overloading have on fluid power and electrical systems?

a] electrical components get damaged in electrical systems

b] fluid power system stops working without damaging the components

c] both a] and b]

d] none of the above

192) How is power transmitted in fluid power systems?

a] power is transmitted instantaneously

b] power is transmitted gradually

c] both a] and b]

d] none of the above

INDUSTRIAL TRAINING INSTITUTE

Monthly Test-12, Marks- 20, Date:- ______________

(Every Question Carry Two Marks)

193) Generally liquids are non-compressible but when a large pressure of 70 bar is applied, petroleum oil can be compressed up to

a] 0]5% of its original volume

b] 1% of its original volume

c] 5% of its original volume

d] none of the above

194) The resistance offered to the flow of fluid inside a piston develops into

a] pressure

b] force

c] stress

d] all of the above

195) At low pressures, liquids are

a] compressible

b] non-compressible

c] unpredictable

196) In hydraulic systems,

a] the mechanical energy is transferred to the oil and then converted into mechanical energy

b] the electrical energy is transferred to the oil and then converted into mechanical energy

c] the mechanical energy is transferred to the oil and converted into electrical energy

d] none of the above

197) Which of the following is used as a component in hydraulic power unit?

a] pressure gauge

b] filler gauge

c] valve

d] reservoir

198) Rotary motion in a hydraulic power unit is achieved by using

a] hydraulic cylinder

b] pneumatic cylinder

c] both hydraulic and pneumatic cylinder

d] none of the above

199) What is the relation between speed and flow rate for fixed displacement vane pump?

a] flow rate increases with increase in speed of rotor

b] flow rate decreases with increase in speed of rotor

c] flow rate is constant and does not change with change in speed

d] none of the above

200) In fixed displacement vane pump,

a] flow rate decreases with increase in working pressure

b] flow rate increases with increase in working pressure

c] flow rate is constant and does not change with working pressure

d] none of the above

201) Which type of motion is transmitted by hydraulic actuators?

a] linear motion

b] rotary motion

c] both a] and b]

d] none of the above

202) What is the function of electric actuator?

a] converts electrical energy into mechanical torque

b] converts mechanical torque into electrical energy

c] converts mechanical energy into mechanical torque

d] none of the above

9 798887 047355

Printed by Libri Plureos GmbH in Hamburg,
Germany